Who Cares?

*Creating a Culture of Service
in your Business*

Scott A. Brown

www.ServiceWithPurpose.com

Savadel Business Services
P.O. Box 121
Sharon Center, Ohio 44274
scott@sbservicepro.com

This publication is designed to provide accurate and authoritative information in regard to the subject matter covered. It is sold with the understanding that neither the author nor the publisher is engaged in rendering legal, accounting, or other professional service. If legal advice or other expert assistance is required, the services of a competent professional person should be sought.
-From a Declaration of Principles jointly adopted by a Committee of the American Bar Association and a Committee of Publishers

Additional copies of *Who Cares? Creating a Culture of Service in your Business* are available at special quantity discounts for use in training programs, incentives or promotions. For more information, please write to Savadel Business Services at the address above or visit www.ServicewithPurpose.com.

Who Cares?
Creating a Culture of Service in your Business
Scott Brown (author)

Editor: Marcie Price, J & M Business Solutions, LLC
jmbs@core.com

ISBN 0-9719079-9-4

Businesspeople give rave reviews for *Who Cares?*

"A true hands-on approach to hospitality that should be used in every aspect of life."

> *– Janet Miller, Training Coordinator*
> *Cleveland Metroparks Zoo*

"Scott's book was a good inspiration to me to revitalize our commitment to customer service!!"

> *– Jordan Owens, President*
> *Danly IEM*

"This book is great. Even reminded an old dog like me things I forgot. You have a gift for writing in layman's terms. I am looking forward to book #2."

> *– John "Lil John" Rinaldi, Owner*
> *Rinaldi's Jewelers*

"This is the best book on customer service I've read in a long time. Every manager should read it."

> *– Carole Sjolander, Executive Director*
> *Int'l Association for the Leisure & Entertainment Industry*

Preface

Hundreds of books have been written extolling the benefits of providing outstanding customer service. But for most of us, we already know that service can pay big dividends for a business. The trick is uncovering why outstanding service happens and discovering the process to make it happen for your business. Although there is no magic formula that instantly makes "customer loyalty" your middle name, there are things that must be done if you ever hope to achieve service greatness. The keys to unlock this greatness are found in the *Six Essentials of Service*, which will be revealed to you in this book.

Who Cares? may not be the only customer service book you'll ever read, but it will change the way you think about all of the business books you've already read and those you have yet to read.

Who Cares? is different because it starts (and finishes) with a plain and simple, long forgotten foundation to help you develop an unforgettable customer service program based around the Six Essentials of Service that will leave your competition scratching their heads as your business and career soar to new heights.

Whether you are an owner, a manager, or even a department of one, *Who Cares?* will serve as your definitive customer service guidebook not only for your customer service department, but for everything you do.

No matter what you do for a living, in some way, you are serving others. *Who Cares?* will give meaning to ordinary actions and transactions and allow you to provide *"Service with Purpose"* to your employees, your vendors and your customers. The concepts in this book are timeless and simple, but when they are combined, the results they produce are incredible. Just as individual ingredients won't make a gourmet meal, the individual disciplines in this book won't serve you nearly as well individually as they will when they are all properly combined together.

Before getting started there are a few things you should know about this book. If you like your business books packed with fancy, scientific-sounding words and dozens of Ivy League research studies – you're not going to find them here (at least not too many of 'em). *Who Cares?* is written in good ol' plain English about a subject that has unfortunately become increasingly complicated. Not here. We won't get anywhere near high tech. The *Service with Purpose* philosophy is a high-touch, personal, one-on-one approach to business. Nothing complicated.

Many of the examples and anecdotes included in this book are derived from the retail, hospitality and service industries. This wasn't done because the book was written exclusively for them. It was done this way because we are all exposed to restaurants, hotels, grocery stores and other retail locations on a daily basis. We can all understand and relate to customer service at this level. But no matter what industry you work in , the ideas, strategies and philosophies can be adapted to help you achieve the level of service to which you aspire.

Scott Brown
October 2003

Table of Contents

Table of Contents *continued*

Introduction:

Okay, so I've got something to say about Customer Service... Who doesn't?

Our world is driven by information. Hundreds of thousands of new book titles, newspapers and magazine articles discuss the latest trends in business and the Internet contains more information than can be comprehended. It seems as though everybody has something to say. It has become relatively easy to have your voice be heard, and with the business world more competitive than ever and business owners and managers continually looking for anything to give them a slight advantage in the marketplace or maybe even to help them survive, many who feel they have something to say have found an audience eager to listen.

So with each passing year, new customer service philosophies are paraded onto the bookshelves. Over time, the concept of customer service has been broken into smaller and smaller pieces until unfortunately, you have nothing left but pieces and no solid foundation.

There's little debate that customer service is currently not very good – to put it mildly. The irony of the whole bad service situation is that there are tons of "self-help" customer service books and most business owners and managers *want* to provide great service to their customers. And yet it's just not getting done. Again, among other things, one of the reasons is that there is no foundation, just those darn pieces-parts.

An additional problem is that many of these customer service books are written from one of two perspectives. First, they are written to "convince" business managers and owners that customer service is both worthwhile and profitable by presenting tons of statistics and anecdotes about the positive impact of quality service. These books are often "preaching to the choir." The people that choose to read them already know *why* service is important and don't need to be convinced about its importance. But they are looking for ways to make their employees care about service as much as they do. If you've ever been a manager for at least ten minutes, then you know that that's not always an easy task. Which is why I'm amused by the customer service books that list example after example of the author's bad customer service experiences. The books always end with the author saying, "If only Company X had done this or that, they would've been superstars. But instead it was a service nightmare." Wow, there's a news flash "service stinks!" But pointing out the problems doesn't necessarily reveal the solutions.

The second type of book is often designed to motivate and give tips to the individual reader on *how* to deliver extraordinary service on a personal level. It provides ways to impress your customers and exceed their expectations with individual acts of greatness. But again, these books are usually motivating the motivated. I know it may happen from time to time, but how many of your front-line employees are walking around with a copy of *Raving Fans* by Ken Blanchard? Answer: Not Enough. The problem is that an owner or manager who is convinced in the value of outstanding customer service and a minimum wage, front-line worker delivering outstanding service are two very, very different things.

Most books separate the "why" from the "how." *"Who Cares?"* is going to pull it all together. You'll not only strengthen your belief in power of great service, you'll be able to build a business that is filled with people wanting to provide the kind of service you've always dreamed of. Pretty exciting, huh?

Don't get me wrong; many of the current articles and books written are right on target, although they often represent only pieces of the whole customer service puzzle. Many businesses and managers simply forge ahead grasping at the latest technology, terminology or fad to fix their service woes and ignore the basic foundation on which effective customer service must be built.

With all of these individual pieces demanding your attention, it becomes very difficult to see the whole picture. And without the whole picture, you'll never be able to provide world-class service to your customers.

As far as having something to say and having a few ideas on how to achieve world-class service, I guess I am no different. But instead of forging ahead with just another piece of the puzzle, I'd like to take a step back so we can see the "big picture." Once we uncover the big picture, we can begin looking at the individual pieces that make up that picture and the way they all fit together. Before we are finished we will cover not only the "why" of customer service, but just as importantly, the "how."

So, if you'll take that big step back with me now, I'd like to share some of those foundational ideas that have gotten lost along the way and some powerful ways to apply them to your business. So here we go on our journey to world-class customer service.

"All glory comes from daring to begin."

- Eugene F. Ware

Chapter 1:

The Foundation of Customer Service

Business is about people.

There you have it. Basically, that's it - that's everything. So what do you think?

...All right, hold on. Don't close the book yet. Is that statement overly simplistic? Absolutely. But more importantly, is it often overlooked when discussing customer service or just about any other aspect of business? Definitely.

I'm not really sure that most people believe that business *is* about people. Most people would probably say business is about making money or selling a product or service. If that was their guess, they wouldn't necessarily be wrong, but they would need to dig deeper if they really wanted to find the most correct answer. Remember this...

No matter what you do, your customers (people) have to hand the money over to you before you ever make a single cent.

People and business cannot be separated. It may be a hard concept for you to swallow at this point but if you always remember that business is about people first and (gulp!) making money second – you will always give yourself the best opportunity to win. If you're not buying it yet, read on and it may become more palatable for you.

So who are these people who are so important to your business anyway?

You know people – all kinds of people: your family, your friends, your neighbors, your business associates. These people have a name you know and a recognizable face and even a personal relationship attached to them. How many of your customers do you know this well? Of course you don't have to be dear friends with everyone you do business with; but if no personal connections exist, it becomes very easy to condemn your customers to a cold database that spits out chunks of information about buying habits and market trends.

Do you really consider your customers to be people? How about friends? Again, you don't have to know them all personally, but how do you *think* of them? Do you care about them beyond the fact that they spend their money with you? According to Jeffrey Gitomer, author of *Customer Satisfaction is Worthless, Customer*

Loyalty is Priceless, "All things being equal, people want to do business with their friends. All things being not quite so equal, people still want to do business with their friends."

How many friends do you do business with?

"All lasting business is built on friendship."
-Alfred A. Montapert

Your discussions of customers may include "levels of satisfaction," market share and per capita spending, but do you honestly ever just talk about or think about the people who use your product or service just as…well…people? Do you ever think of them without percentage signs attached to them? Most businesses don't, and that's a huge mistake.

Being the outstanding businessperson you are, you certainly know these people as they relate to your bottom line. You know these people as the entities that want your products, that buy your products, that tell their friends about your products, and that occasionally call you up to complain about your products. You know them as dollar signs and coupon return rates and by all other forms of statistical analysis. But do you honestly have any idea who they are? Do you care?

Wait a second… Aha! We've uncovered our foundation. THE FOUNDATION OF ALL CUSTOMER SERVICE! (Can you hear the dramatic music in the background?)

If business is about people, then…

CUSTOMER SERVICE IS:

Caring about the people you do business with.

Ah, there it is, our foundation! Now we're really getting somewhere! Caring about others is an idea as old as time, and a business strategy more powerful than any new age business philosophy.

See, this is simple stuff!

Please be warned! If you like the complexity that has become commonplace in business today, or if you think it takes a Ph.D. to become an outstanding business person or if your stomach turns at a naïve idea like "caring" as an effective business strategy, then please do not read any further.

...Are you still there?

If you're skeptical but you choose to read on, keep an open mind. If you've already decided that anyone who thinks that caring is the secret weapon to service has an overly simplistic view of business, don't worry. I'm not going to spend all of my time trying to convince you to adopt a caring approach to your business. This book is written for those who are open to the idea and are looking for not only financial gains in their business, but also a sense of fulfillment and contribution in their personal lives. Who isn't looking for that?

Some readers may find that this book is not for them – too much of this touchy-feely emotional stuff. If someone feels that way it's unfortunate, because in my opinion, caring is not simply an option for your company, it's a necessity – the foundation on which your company should be built.

This foundation of caring is what I call *Service with Purpose*. The concept of *Service with Purpose* is about understanding the importance of customer service not only for a business' financial success, but also for the personal satisfaction that you, your employees and your customers deserve from a business relationship. It's knowing that what you do truly matters.

This caring approach to business is not unique to *Service with Purpose*. In fact, some of the country's most highly regarded companies have already embraced a caring business philosophy. For example, if you worked at Walt Disney World you might call this caring approach "creating magic" or "spreading a little pixie dust." In the case of Disney, these cute-sounding terms have created a giant in the entertainment industry and the benchmark of service excellence. Point being, don't allow the simplicity of the terms and concepts in this book to detract from their ability to generate new levels of profitability and a powerful, competitive advantage for you.

"I Like Money!"

Basing your business on a foundation of caring does not mean you're oblivious to making money. Nothing could be further from the truth. After all, making money is probably one of the main reasons you became a part of the business world. I enjoy making money, and hopefully you do, too. Unless you want to work for a social service organization, making money should be important to you. Even non-profit organizations are trying to make a profit for their cause.

Of course, it's wonderful to provide excellent service just because it's the right thing to do and you get "warm fuzzies" every time you read a thank you note from a devoted customer. But the bottom line does count. That's the good news because applying a *Service with Purpose* approach to your business will allow you to do what's right – and give your business a competitive advantage at the same time.

If you believe that this just might make sense, that's great. But philosophy alone cannot – will not – get it done. The belief also needs specific actions to make it happen. In upcoming chapters we will introduce and discuss how working through the Six Essentials of Service will create and maintain a *Service with Purpose* business.

"Caring is the key."

– Brian Tracy

Chapter 2:

I Don't Care

If you don't care about people, it is IMPOSSIBLE to provide world-class customer service.

Strong words, and of course in this life there are no absolutes. In business especially, there are no such things as "always" and "never." You very well may know a "successful" businessperson who cares only about himself. I know some exist. Like the character Scrooge in *A Christmas Carol*, you can have financial gain without caring about the people around you.

Most likely this type of person works independently – or at least they should. They are accountable to no one but themselves and aren't really interested in the social merits of their business pursuits or what others think about them. Years of profits and financial gain will sound good to some, even if they have to step on a few toes along the way. So for the purpose of this book, "success" will not be defined by mere profits, but also by the contributions you and your company make to improve the lives of your customers and employees and the sense of satisfaction you get from doing what you do.

For those who define success solely by the amount of money they accumulate, there will unfortunately come a day when their business reaches a plateau or when strong competition comes into the market and they will lose. Maybe not all at once, but it will happen. Maybe the losses won't be financial. These losses may be more personal or even spiritual when they discover that making money in and of itself is a shallow pursuit – the same way that Scrooge realized how empty his life was, not because he wasn't a good businessman or didn't have tons of money, but because he didn't care about anyone beside himself.

> ### *"A business that makes nothing but money is a poor kind of business."*
> -Henry Ford

Now that I think about it, this may be a good time for you to put this book down, go check out *A Christmas Carol* at your library, read it, and then get back to this book… Well, maybe you can do that later – or just rent the DVD. Regardless, it seems like Charles Dickens would be a strong proponent of *Service with Purpose*.

Of course the example of *A Christmas Carol* is about one man's business practices. One man who most certainly had no interest in customer service. He had no compassion for his only employee, his customers or the human race in general. Since you've chosen to read a book about customer service, you've probably already realized that the modern world of service leaves little room for someone like Scrooge. Whether you're the newest front-line employee or a manager or owner, if you truly care only about yourself, your career will never reach its full potential.

Let's carry the Christmas theme one step further with the movie, *A Miracle on 34th Street.* Just in case you're the only person in the world who hasn't seen this movie, it's the one where a department store Santa sends customers to other department stores to find what they need. (There are other parts to the movie as well… they think Santa's crazy… he goes to court… I guess you'll have to watch that DVD, too.)

The point I'm trying to make is, would you send your potential customers somewhere else if one of your competitors could better serve them? It wouldn't be easy to do, but just as in the movie, people will begin to come to you first. You'll become a trusted friend – someone who cares – as opposed to just a supplier of goods and services.

There is no business practice in the world that is more sound and effective than basing your business on a foundation of caring. However, very few businesses would even consider "caring" as a business practice. This fact leaves the floor open for you to amaze your customers and even your competitors' customers when you dazzle them with your caring ways. But before you embrace this philosophy and expect to find yourself in business utopia, beware of this addendum as well:

Just because you care about people does not mean you will succeed in business.

Sad but true. Sometimes nice people go out of business. If your business is not fundamentally sound with a strong financial backing, excellent products, strong marketing and an unrelenting desire to win, you may not succeed. Rest assured, though, that whatever shortcomings your business may have, there is no stronger remedy than taking care of your customers better than anyone else ever could.

Lawrence Steinmetz, author of *How to Sell at Prices Higher than your Competitors*, suggests that there are basically five ways to develop a competitive edge in business. His list includes:

√   Price
√   Quality
√   Advertising/Promotions
√   Delivery
√   Service

Each one of these items are obviously worth your attention and can impact the success of your business; but for my money, the others do not have the same long-term impact as service. For example, we know that customers are willing to pay more for a similar product because of the superior service or personal attention they receive at one business over another.

Secondly, although advertising, promotions and discounts can bring "shoppers" into your business, it is your service, your personal connection, that turns shoppers into loyal customers. Your service can turn that coupon-clipping bargain hunter into someone who spends her money with you for years to come.

Lastly, your competitors cannot duplicate your human resources. If business is about people, then service is definitely the one item on that list that is directly impacted by the people that represent your business. I believe that two of the items on that list – quality and delivery – are also part of your service culture. Start with service and everything else will fall into place.

Chapter 3:

Why Is Customer Service So Bad?

As we've discussed, the amount of information about customer service is staggering. Everybody thinks they know everything there is to know about customer service. Remember you really do know everything there is to know about customer service... (You didn't forget already, did you?) Customer service is caring about the people you do business with.

Got it? Good!

Whether or not it is understood or even taken seriously, it is generally believed in the business world that good customer service is important. In reality, believing that customer service is important is about as far as most businesses take the concept. They acknowledge that service is important, and then hurry back to the "real" parts of running their businesses.

No business person in his right mind would publicly claim he doesn't care about service. And yet if you've done business with anyone, anywhere, you've probably noticed that there are quite a few businesses that really don't care about you or about serving you – they just want your money. Ironically, when they don't treat you well, not only will they not see you again, they won't see your money again either!

Publicly, most businesspeople feel very comfortable in claiming that they do indeed provide excellent customer service. Companies will hang banners, have it printed on their employees' shirts, promote it in their advertising, and on it goes. If you ask business owners or managers about customer service, most could expound for hours on the importance of customer service and the ways in which their business has become a service leader in their field. In fact, you'd probably have a hard time finding a business that doesn't claim to hold "excellent service" as one of its primary goals.

So with all the attention that is given to customer service, why is service so regularly bad and more often horrible? The answer is that most people actually DON'T know that much about customer service. They simply agree with the *concept* of customer service. And beyond that, how many businesses even *acknowledge* having "caring" as a part of their business culture? This in itself is a cause of service breakdowns.

Think of just about any service problem that you have personally suffered through. Nearly every service failure stems from either a lack of caring from the business itself, its procedures or an individual who represents that business.

Was it a rude waiter? Was it someone who continually recited policy even though it didn't apply to your situation? Was it a business that made it impossible to speak with a real live person to help you solve your problem? When individuals or businesses don't care about their customers (even unintentionally), service suffers. Caring makes all the difference in the world.

Recently I went to a toy store at a local mall to buy a handheld video game for my daughter for her birthday. I hadn't bought a game like that for 15 years, so I was somewhat out of the loop as far as what games were good and so on. Before I left the house I wrote down a few basic questions to ask, to make sure that I was buying the right system.

The store was busy when I arrived, so I waited in line for my turn to speak to the 16-year-old cashier. I explained my situation and told the cashier that I had a few questions for her. She said, "Okay."

I asked her my first question and she shook her head and said, "I dunno."

I presented her with my second question. "Nope. No idea," she said frankly. I could see she had already grown tire of my questions. Keep in mind that behind this cashier was a wall filled from top to bottom with these games – obviously a big seller for the company she was working for.

Undaunted, I tried one more question and received the same irritated, negative response.

The line was growing longer behind me, but she just stood there and stared at me as if daring me to ask another question. I wouldn't give her the pleasure, so I just stood there and stared right back at her. We were both trying to make each other feel awkward. Actually, it was kind of fun.

Finally, I just left and bought the game at another store.

Do you think this cashier was infused with a *Service with Purpose* attitude? It really wasn't her fault – or at least it wasn't only her fault. Great customer service strategies are taught and lived – so are bad ones.

From this day on, make sure you're accountable for the level of service your company, department or team provides. Don't assume everyone knows how to treat a customer, because they don't. If you hire just anybody off the street, provide five minutes of training and then slap a new company T-shirt or stylish smock on their back, don't even think about blaming them for your company's horrible service.

One of the problems is that the importance of having happy customers and customer friendly policies and employees seems like only a matter of common sense. And since everyone believes they have common sense (a notion that can certainly be debated), they conclude that they have a complete understanding of all the issues involving customer service. When companies have service break-downs, they blame it on the "dumb kids working the register" or the "idiot customer." Never does the blame fall on the managers or the business policies they developed. How could it? They understand customer service completely. It's their customer who doesn't know what they're talking about.

Now don't lose faith. There are those who do provide ex-cellent service, and even they may find it difficult to give a simple answer to explain exactly what they do to provide that service. That's because, whether they know it or not, companies that are service leaders care about their customers – and they care about their em-ployees, as well. They understand that true customer service is not a department within their business; it is a philosophy that permeates it. Just as you cannot script out every aspect of a caring relationship, you cannot completely script out outstanding customer service. Great service is fluid and will change and mature over time. It's interactive. It's alive. It's part of who you are as a business.

"It's sometimes difficult to separate natural human kindness from customer service. Exceptional customer service does not grow out of a set of hard-and-fast rules – it's a consistent way of doing business that domes from the heart.."

– Debra J. Schmidt

As I said at the very beginning, understanding the foundation of customer service is imperative. And that's what I've tried to help you do so far. Its importance cannot be overstated.

Sure, there are many benefits to developing and maintaining a *Service with Purpose* business, but what if you just don't have time for all of this service stuff? Do you really lose anything by not providing quality service?

Chapter 4:

What Is the Cost of BAD Service?

Jill Griffin, author of *Customer Service: How to Earn It, How to Keep It*, states that the average company in America today loses, at minimum, 20 percent of its customers every year. For many companies, customer losses are even higher. Another report from the Harvard Business Review figures that, on average, businesses lose 50 percent of their customers every five years. These customer losses may occur for many reasons, but studies show that nearly 70 percent of the customers that stop doing business with you do so because of poor or indifferent service.

These losses, which are mainly caused by poor service and, indirectly, from a lack of caring, come with a huge price tag. Do the math. You know (or should know) how much your customers spend and how often they visit or buy from you. Multiply that out over three, five or even ten years. How much are you potentially losing? Yikes!

The good news is that you can reclaim that money by *keeping* your customers. Bain & Co., a leading business research firm, determined that when companies retain just 5 percent more of their best customers, profits can be boosted 25 to 85 percent, depending on the industry. The lifetime value of customers comes largely from their repeat business and referrals, not from their first purchase. Keep your customers coming back. Great service pays and it pays well.

Honestly, how much more information do you need? All right, here's a little more.

It costs 6 times more to acquire new customers than it does to keep the ones you already have.

Besides that…word of mouth advertising is 50 times more powerful than regular advertising. It is estimated that more than 50 percent of purchasing in America is stimulated by these free word-of-mouth ads. Get people talking about how great you are!

It boils down to either keeping the your current customers happy or going out to find new ones. Continually finding new customers is a very expensive proposition and at some point the well will run dry.

Chapter 5:

A Benefit of Great Service

Consumers have come to expect that just about anything they purchase at a reasonable price should be of a decent quality. There are not tremendous differences from one product to another. It's not like the days when a "Made in Japan" sticker let you know that you were buying something of inferior quality.

Today, people expect the things they buy to work properly or taste good, and to meet their needs no matter what or where they buy. This is especially true with technology products like cell phones, televisions, computers or stereo equipment. Whether it is true or not, people generally feel that they'll be happy with whatever they purchase.

When customers believe that products purchased from different companies are essentially the same, retailers begin treating these products like mere commodities. From cutting prices to flashy promotions, retailers will do anything to get customers through their doors. This is a lowest-price-wins mentality, and although the consumer benefits in this situation, the retailer loses. If your only claim to fame is that you have the lowest prices in town, what happens when someone appears in your market with lower prices than you? Your future ad campaign of "We *Almost* Have the Lowest Prices in Town!" doesn't have quite the same ring.

How do you stay out of this mess? Provide better service than anyone else. And when I say "anyone else" I don't just mean your competitors, I mean anyone else that your customer may come in contact with. No, I'm not crazy. For example, name some of the "biggies" in customer service. What are some of the names that pop into your mind? Disney, FedEx, Nordstrom, the Ritz-Carlton? What do these businesses have in common besides customer service? Not much, and yet they are grouped together because of their service excellence. Great service is great service no matter what your line of work. Again, don't just compare yourself to your direct competitors. If you do, you will be limiting your opportunities for improvement.

Still, how do you stay out of a price war? Answer: Charge more for what you do. No, I'm still not crazy. Know this fact:

People are willing to pay for service.

No, they're not willing to pay for your *claims* of service or your slogans that extol the virtues of service. In fact, I've really come to resent companies that throw around their service slogans and have no desire to back them up. These empty promises are paraded on radio and television daily. "Service is our most important job!" "We're here for you when you need us."

It sounds good, but when you visit their location, you find that it's filled with the same disinterested, unmotivated people that you can find anywhere else. If you can't deliver service, don't even mention it. That only makes it worse.

But if you *can* deliver the service you promise, your customers will be willing to pay to have their expectations regularly exceeded and to know that they are truly appreciated.

Chapter 6:

Don't Wait
for the Bandwagon,
It Starts with YOU

As you're reading and absorbing this information, you should find yourself getting a little excited as you begin to understand the power of applying a *Service with Purpose* philosophy to everything you do. Whether you're a front-liner, a regional manager, or the CEO – a *Service with Purpose* attitude pays off!

Nothing will kill your team's energy faster than holding a big meeting and enthusiastically announcing your new "customer focus plan." Then, two weeks later... nothing has changed.

If you're in a management position, be prepared for skepticism and even silent ridicule from subordinates and co-workers alike as you begin to introduce your new *Service with Purpose* philosophies. "Here we go again," your employees will think to themselves, even if they're not brave enough to speak the words aloud. They've seen and heard it all before. They expect that in a few weeks this initiative will begin to fizzle and fade away. Until you show them something by taking some distinctive and consistent actions your employees are going to be hesitant to jump on the bandwagon.

To build a *Service with Purpose* culture, be ready personally to shoulder the responsibility that is required to establish the belief and enthusiasm of your employees and customers. Over time, you will build your *Service with Purpose* bandwagon that will be en route to world-class service.

Eventually, a *Service with Purpose* business will generate energy through the support and enthusiasm of the entire team. But until that happens, it's up to you.

When you begin working through the Six Essentials of Service, don't get discouraged if things don't move as quickly as you had hoped, because they seldom do. Definitely don't get discouraged when things don't work perfectly the way you had planned, because they *never* do. Just be consistent in your efforts and the results will be astounding.

 Consistency...
        Consistency...
                Consistency.

> *"Striving for excellence motivates you; striving for perfection demoralizes you."*
>
> -Harriet Braiker

Remember, just as with anything that has any true value in our lives, you get out of it what you put into it. Don't just toss a few copies of this book around and expect the ideas to take root and turn your business into a customer service leader. Unfortunately, things that are worthwhile don't work like that.

In addition to the belief and energy you will supply, there are a few more requirements to initiate your *Service with Purpose* program successfully. If you're the owner of the company, the following should go without mention. But regardless of your role, make sure you exemplify the following characteristics.

Requirements to Successfully Initiate a *Service with Purpose* Program

√   Have the "Attitude of Ownership."
√   Believe in what you're doing.
√   Be willing to put in the needed effort.
√   Believe in your products or services.
√   Understand the value of service.
√   Get people involved in the process.

You first need to start with the right attitude. Always have the "Attitude of Ownership." Whether you're the newest front-line employee or the CEO, it is *your* business. Treating your job with an owner's attitude will give you a competitive edge both within your company and with the outside competition. Along with the Attitude of Ownership, you also must believe in the products or services that your business offers. Whether your company excels in price, quality, service or efficiency – or some combination, find out what makes your business and products special and embrace them.

Additionally, you must understand the true value of service. That is, service to your customers and service to your employees. Hopefully, you've already come to understand the value of service. If not – there's always page one and this time I'll write slower for you. But if you are enjoying success and personal fulfillment with your job or company, you most likely have already adopted many of these principles. The *Service with Purpose* program will simply maximize your efforts.

Lastly, get people involved at every opportunity and at every level. As we'll discuss in Chapter 13, communication is extremely important. Ask your co-workers, managers and even your customers what improvements they'd like to see. Listen to what people have to say. When the people around you know that you're sincerely interested in what they have to say, you're much more likely to have their support as you begin to build your *Service with Purpose* company.

A *Service with Purpose* philosophy will work within any type of business structure. The most important element is you - someone who cares enough to start making a difference.

Chapter 7:

Creating a *Service with Purpose* Culture

Now we're really getting somewhere. By now, you believe that building a business on a foundation of caring is not only the right thing to do, but is also profitable and the most powerful tool in your arsenal against your competition and an ever-changing market.

If you're prepared, I am now going to reveal the individual disciplines that are required to create a *Service with Purpose* business. The pieces are called the Six Essentials of Service. These disciplines are non-negotiable. You cannot pick and choose the essentials of service that you feel are important and dismiss the rest as overkill or unnecessary. You do have some flexibility, though. Even though suggestions are provided on how to maximize each essential, you ultimately decide how things will work best for you and your business. Control remains in your hands at all times.

The success of *Service with Purpose* is dependent upon you consistently and consciously working on each discipline.

Become a Great Business Chef

You may be disappointed to find that there is no official rulebook that must be followed. Everyone's application of *Service with Purpose* is going to be their own. You will start with a common philosophy and adapt it to your business. This is not a "turnkey" process. The Six Essentials are more like the ingredients necessary to make a gourmet meal. Although quality ingredients will make the meal possible, it's up to the chef to bring it all together. Welcome to the kitchen!

The Six Essentials of Service aren't intended to conveniently pack service into a neat little box. It simply doesn't work that way. If it did – everyone would provide great service. In fact, the more you understand the foundation of service, the further the reach of service stretches throughout your business. Service becomes all-encompassing. Customer service must touch every corner of every aspect of your business. It must be the essence of everything you do.

The Six Essentials of Service bring your beliefs and actions together. They're about creating a culture of service. Service for your employees, your customers, your vendors, and for everyone associated with your company. The Six Essentials of Service is how it all works.

Okay, it's time! Here comes the meat and potatoes you've been waiting for!

Chapter 8:

The Three P's of Service

The remainder of this book will cover the "how's" of service – all of the things that must be done to create a *Service with Purpose* culture in your business. As we've already discussed, simply believing in the power of a caring business approach is not enough. Anybody can talk the talk (most people do), but very, very few people walk the walk. By utilizing the Six Essentials of Service to create a *Service with Purpose* business you WILL walk the walk.

But before we dive head first into the Six Essentials, I need to tell you about the Three P's of Service. The Three P's of Service are the "guts" of the Six Essentials - the inner workings. Don't worry, it doesn't get any more complicated than that.

Just like your own guts, everyone knows that they've got them, but they don't want to see them. When they're working well you don't even know they're there, and when they go bad they impact everything else. From time to time you may need to do things differently to maintain your guts (i.e. change your diet, exercise, etc.) to keep things running smoothly. Is this clarifying things for you or just grossing you out?

What are the Three P's you wonder?

√ **Planning**
√ **Procedures**
√ **People**

In business, everything you do, whether you're consciously aware of it or not, involves planning, procedures and people. The three are inextricably linked. The success or failure of one impacts the other two. For example, the strength of your employees' personal skills can overcome a bad policy or procedure, if they know how to handle your customers. Conversely, great procedures can make an average bunch of employees very efficient.

Consistent service success depends on all three of these items being successfully in place. The words themselves are pretty clear and self-explanatory and make up the process that creates the service culture.

From this point on, don't make any final decisions without running your options through the Three P's of Service.

To create a *Service with Purpose* culture, each and every one of the Six Essentials of Service must be an active, living part of your plan.

Chapter 9:

The Pieces Parts –
The Six Essentials of Service

As you read through the Six Essentials of Service, you may find that you are already familiar with each of the individual elements that are required to create your *Service with Purpose* program. Despite your familiarity, I encourage you to continually work to improve your abilities in each of these areas. You may already be very proficient in some of the essentials. Others may need some work. And with some you may need to start from square one. This is the case for most businesses. They have strengths in some areas and are weaker in others. Ignoring or being unaware of your service strengths and weaknesses is a typical cause of service breakdowns. The Six Essentials will fill the gaps and keep it all tied together.

This book should be your launch pad to achieving excellence in each one of the essentials that separate the great from the merely good. The key is that each of the essentials is required in order to achieve success. Take none of them lightly. They all work together like a circuit. Remove one and the circuit is broken.

If you would like more information on any of the Six Essentials of Service, rest assured that each one has already been written about, discussed and dissected hundreds of times over. For your sake and mine, I'm not going to try to outdo what has already been done. I encourage you to continue to study the information that is out there regarding each one of the essentials we will review.

There is no pick and choose, no taking only what you want. This isn't a buffet. All of the principles must be alive and well for you to succeed. Have I beaten the dead horse enough? Good.

Now, let's move on to the first essential of service.

The Six Essentials of Service

1 - Vision

2 -

3 -

4 -

5 -

6 -

Chapter 10:

Essential #1

Vision

"The only limits are, as always, those of vision."
-James Broughton

Creating your vision. This is where we begin to plan something fantastic... Now sit back and relax. Close your eyes... You're getting sleepy... You're getting veeery sleepy...

Now imagine everything in your company or department looking and working perfectly. Imagine all of those happy customers. There are lots of 'em! They're buying everything they can from you! Depending on the type of business you have, your customers may be visiting your clean, inviting store or restaurant, or they may be visiting your web site or calling you to place an order. Your customers are continually telling their friends about you. Of course, all of your employees are motivated and enthusiastic. Your systems are all running smoothly and you didn't forget a thing. Wow! Now that's a day at work!

Now when I click my fingers you will awaken... click!

Wasn't that nice? Don't you feel refreshed and invigorated?

Okay, now back to reality. As we all know, perfection is an impossible goal, but it is a worthwhile target and it certainly doesn't hurt to dream.

When planning your vision, it's your time to dream and plan, to see things the way you'd like them to be. From there, you can develop and put the procedures and people in place to make your vision a reality. Creating your Vision is really all about the "planning" portion of the 3 P's. See things the way you want them to be. Don't let yourself get bogged down; you'll have plenty of time to work out all of the details. Obviously, envisioning everything the way you'd like it to be is a huge chunk to bite off. So where do you start?

Here's the critical question to ask yourself as you begin laying out your vision. What are you planning for? What is your vision all about? Do you have an answer? Of course you do! You're planning the development of a caring, service-based business that kicks your competitors' butts – right? Right!

Where Should You Begin?

If you're looking for ideas on caring, start at the source. Start with you! Begin with your definition of caring as you see it through the people you care about and who care about you. List the attitudes and actions that you feel would be essential to a caring relationship with your family or friends.

As an example, I have created a list of "Ten Things That People Who Care about You Will Do." This is my list of caring attributes. It is in no particular order and is only ten of the hundreds (or possibly thousands) of items that you could add to the list. Imagine each one of these caring attributes being preceded by the statement, "People who care about you will…"

Ten Things That People Who Care about You Will Do

1.   Look out for your best interests.
2.   Treat you with fairness, openness and honesty.
3.   Be sincerely glad to see you.
4.   Go out of their way to make sure you're happy and well taken care of.
5.   Forgive you when you've made a mistake.
6.   Let you know how much you are appreciated.

7.   Keep you in their plans.

8.   Keep you updated on what's happening in their lives and be interested in what's happening in yours.

9.   Invite you over every once in a while.

10. Be there when you need them.

Keep in mind, this list was created using my definitions of caring with regard to *personal* relationships. By glancing over the list, it should become clear that all of these elements transfer over to business relationships incredibly well. Caring is caring. No matter what you do – with some minor variations – this simple list of ten caring attributes can apply to your business.

Now think of the places where you do business. How many caring attributes do you think they practice? Any? In terms of your business, if you do nothing more than think of service through your own caring attributes, you will dramatically impact the way you do business. As I've said from the beginning, this isn't a new philosophy – it's incredibly old, but often forgotten. Regardless, there can be no doubt that this concept has been overlooked in terms of a business strategy. It may be too obvious for some, and others may find it too elementary or too simple to be of any real value. Don't believe 'em – it works!

Now it's time for you to do some work. Yea, I know, but there are no free lunches around here. You need to pull your own weight! What you need to do is create your own list and define caring in your own terms. You're welcome to use items from my list, add some of your own or create an entirely new list. Don't think in terms of business yet. Think in terms of your own personal relationships.

The important thing is to find caring attributes that you feel most strongly about. This is critical because it is from this step in the process that all of your other decisions will eventually be made. Take your time, because if you truly believe in your list, the eventual changes in your business and in your career will be profound.

Okay, take a break and work on your list... Seriously – stop reading and work on your list... I've provided the lines – now just fill them in... C'mon! Go ahead... People who care about you will ...

My List of Caring Attributes

1. _____

2. _____

3. _____

4. _____

5. _____

6. _____

7. _____

8. _____

9. _____

10. _____

If you're anything like me, you'll understand why I'll remain rather skeptical on whether you actually worked on your list. But for the sake of argument, we'll assume that you did. If you really have, then the metamorphosis has begun. If not, well, just keep tagging along. As I said, you can use items from my list, but you need to have your brain work through your own definitions. Eventually, we will translate your list of caring attributes into business terms. For now, by simply having a list of caring attributes, you will have the ability to start consciously making decisions from your customers' points of view.

To some extent, I'm sure you already consider your customers' viewpoints in your decision-making process. But the question is, how much weight has it carried in making your final decisions? Were you truly *concerned* about it or were you simply *aware* of it? In the past, what has been the driving factor in your decision-making process? Profits or people? Has it worked? Could it be better?

One way to better deliver your caring attributes to your customers is through "customer points of contact."

Customer Points of Contact

You must be conscious of your customers' total experience when developing your vision. The customers' total experience includes every point at which they interact with your business, from beginning to end – and beyond.

Consider this. How do your expectations change when you walk into a "greasy spoon" versus when you go into a gourmet restaurant? Do you expect to receive a different level of service? Does it change the amount of money you may expect to pay? Do you expect to enjoy a higher quality meal at the gourmet restaurant? Of course you do.

What does your business or department say about you? What types of expectations do your customers have about you? Everything is saying something. From the Yellow Pages advertisement where your customer found your number, to your company's switchboard operator and that dreaded voicemail system, to your store or office location, return policies, store lighting, parking lot convenience, employee demeanor and even the conditions of your restrooms. On and on it goes. Success is found in the details. Pay fanatical attention to detail. While your customers may not notice each and every little thing you do, they will notice that, as a whole, there is something special about your business and how you operate.

Speaking of the condition of your restrooms, what kind of toilet paper do you provide for your customers? The cheap, flimsy, sand-papery stuff or the same kind you would use in your own home? It's not a big deal, you say? You're obviously someone who has never used the sand-papery stuff! It is a big deal. Would your mother let you use the sand-papery stuff? I don't think so. You don't give sand-papery toilet paper to people you care about.

To be 100% on target with your customer service program, *every* point of customer contact must enhance and create synergy with your service vision – not just most of them. You may never receive a thank you letter for the quality of toilet paper you use in your restrooms; but believe me, somewhere out there is a customer who appreciates it very much. One more thing: Don't splurge on toilet paper for your customers and then buy the cheap stuff for your employees.

Beyond toilet paper, here are just a few additional points of contact to consider when developing your vision. Keep in mind there are thousands, so don't let yourself get overwhelmed. This small listing is simply intended to open your mind to the possibilities.

Advertising – What is the message you're promoting? Do you live up to it? How do you present yourself to the public? Look at all of your printed material. Does it look sharp and professional or does it look homemade? Many times, advertising gives your customer his first impression of your business. If you don't advertise in the media, remember that the sign hanging in the front of your business is a form of advertising, too. It all presents an image to your customers and prospective customers.

Phones – Who's answering the phones, a real person or a machine? Is the phone system user-friendly or do you just think it is? How quickly are calls returned? Can the people who answer the phones help the customer or do they just pass them along?

Employees – How do your employees look? Professional? Do they know the answers? Are they well trained? Are they trying to make a difference for themselves and your company or are they just there to make a buck? Following the Six Principles of Service will really help you and your employees succeed by creating a culture of service and a business that not only talks about providing service, but also lives your vision.

Your list of customer contact points can be virtually limitless. Before you get overwhelmed and give up trying to anticipate every point of customer contact, there is a simple, very useful way to make sure you address the key contact points. As an example, go back to the gourmet restaurant mentioned earlier. If you owned this restaurant and wanted to make sure you were aware of your major points of customer contact, you would start by tracking an imaginary customer's visit to your establishment. Your chart could look something like the following:

1. Customer discovers your business by word of mouth, a newspaper advertisement or your yellow pages listing.

2. Customer calls for a reservation. This may be the first human contact the potential customer has with your restaurant.

3. Customer drives to your restaurant and enters the parking lot.

4. Customer has the opportunity to take advantage of valet parking. The first person greeting the customer at your restaurant may be the parking attendant.

5.   Customer enters the lobby and is greeted by the maître d'.

6.   Customer is seated in the dining area and is then greeted by the waiter or waitress. (Are specials suggested, good wines, house specialties?)

7.   Customer places his order.

8.   Food is delivered to the table. (How is the food presented? What is the temperature of the food, overall quality of the meal?)

9.   After the meal, the waiter makes dessert suggestions.

10. The customer completes the meal and pays the bill.

You now have at least ten major customer points of contact that you can focus on for service excellence. As you've already discovered, this list can extend well beyond ten items. But if you can excel at these ten major opportunities, you'll have unprecedented success.

Now let's move away from the imaginary scenario and uncover your own key points of customer contact. Most businesses will probably have somewhere between five and ten points. If you have more or less that's okay. Be sure to create your list from your own point of reference, your sphere of influence. If you only have the authority to control points of customer contact within your department, then list those; if you own the business, you can dictate it all.

My List of Customer Points of Contact

1. _____

2. _____

3. _____

4. _____

5. _____

6. _____

7. _____

8. _____

9. _____

10. _____

Exceeding Expectations

Your points of customer contact provide you with an excellent opportunity to exceed your customers' expectations. You probably already have a good idea as to what your customers expect to happen at your points of contact. Your opportunity to excel occurs when you pinpoint opportunities to provide your customers with what they *don't* expect – in a positive manner of course.

If you own a restaurant, your customers will expect to have a good meal, but they may not expect to receive a free dessert just because you decided that everyone seated at 6 PM on a Tuesday deserves one. Would giving everyone in your restaurant a free dessert exceed their expectations? Absolutely! It would make a dramatic impact on their expectations, and it is this emotional bond that turns satisfied customers into loyal ones.

Make it personal. Some research suggests that true customer loyalty may only exist when an emotional link is developed between the customer and the business. Emotional links can be created when your customers' expectations are exceeded. Do whatever it takes to make your customers' experience with your business a pleasant surprise.

Find ways to surprise and delight your customers at every opportunity. Think out of the box. Come up with as many ideas as you can and implement as many as possible.

When you continually exceed your customers' expectations and treat them better than anyone else, you begin to create a sense of obligation in your customers. Manfred Esser of Customer Loyalty, Ltd., has deemed this sense of obligation "Guilt Marketing." Esser contends that by treating your customers incredibly well – especially your best customers, you create a feeling in them that they would be disloyal to you if they did business with someone else.

Now there's something that doesn't happen very often, having customers feel guilty for not buying from you.

Discovering your Core Beliefs

Before finalizing your vision, remember that every customer defines great customer service differently and that each of his or her definitions is the correct one.

Keep your ears and eyes open at all times. Your customers are giving you hints as to what they like and what they want. Therefore, your vision must be able to adapt to your customers' needs. Tony Alessandra, author of *The Platinum Rule,* points out the Platinum Rule of Customer Service – "Do unto your customers not what you would like, but what they want done unto them."

Now go back and review your list of caring attributes. Some of them may translate perfectly into business terms. Others, like "always kiss my Aunt Fannie when she comes over," may need to be tweaked slightly. But as you sort through and evaluate your list, your business core beliefs will begin to surface.

Your core beliefs will serve as the roadmap for your business. It will guide your employees in their decision making and assure your customers of what they can expect when dealing with your business or your department. These core beliefs will create the unshakable foundation of your service culture and will weave a line of consistency throughout your whole organization.

Planning your Vision will be the birthplace of your Core Beliefs from which all your decisions will be based. When challenges and questions arise, you and your employees can look to your Core Beliefs to find the solutions that'll keep your company on target.

Your vision will be the origin of your core beliefs from which all of your decisions are based. When challenges and questions arise, you and your employees can look to your core beliefs to find the solutions that'll keep you all on target.

Your core beliefs will help to create the unshakable foundation of your service culture and will weave a line of consistency throughout your whole organization.

In order for your customer service program to be effective, you must believe in your core beliefs 100%, unfailingly and with a true sense of passion. That's why I've stressed that my list of caring attributes is indeed, *my* list. These attributes are important to me and may or may not be as important to you.

As I mentioned before, from your list of ten caring attributes, you will develop your own core beliefs. I have taken my list of caring attributes and translated them into some general core belief statements for my speaking and consulting business, as an example. These are some of my "big picture" beliefs. Later we will review some specific examples for a fictitious grocery store. The following are my business core beliefs that were derived from my list of caring attributes:

Core Belief #1: Care for all of your customers - always.

I know that this may seem obvious, and yet it's too important not to address directly. After all, this is what the book is all about. You must *sincerely* care about your customers. And you must care not only about the people that purchase your products or services, but also about your vendors and your *internal* customers – your employees and even your co-workers. If you do everything right, but are simply going through the motions, or see a customer as a necessary evil, you're missing the point entirely.

A service-focused environment can only be created when everyone cares, sincerely cares, about the customer and each other.

Core Belief #2: My business exists for my customers... and for no other reason.

Your products or services are made for the use, convenience and/or enjoyment of your customers. Without them, you have no business. Often, decisions are made based solely on the bottom line or "what's best for the company." Big mistake. What's right for the customer is almost always what's right for the business. When making decisions about your business, you must always very carefully consider the benefits or costs to the customer. Decisions made without the consideration of your customers are at best geared toward short-term gain and most likely will lead to long-term losses.

Core Belief #3: My customers are my partners.

You can't be in business without someone to pay you for what you do. Without customers, you have no business. Work with your customers to maximize the benefits of the relationship for both of you.

Core Belief #4: I think of my customers like family.

This may be my most important belief. If you can think of customers as "family," you can really begin to reap the rewards of a *Service with Purpose* business.

Before you think this "family" stuff is just getting too weird, please allow me to explain. A *Service with Purpose* company is not blind to the obvious or "Pollyanna" in its views. We all know that customers are not always right – or bright – even though they may think otherwise. Your beloved customers are even occasionally obnoxious, extremely hard to please and unappreciative. Now I would bet you, that if you think about it really hard, you could think of one, if not several people, in your immediate family that would fit the same description. For many of us, that could describe our entire family! The thing is, we accept these flaws in our family members (most of them anyway). When we think of our customers as family, we begin not only to accept these character flaws, we also come to expect them.

Granted, thinking of your customers as family can be considered nothing more than semantics, but would you really tell your Aunt

Fannie that she couldn't return the shirt she bought from your store because she bought it more than two weeks ago or didn't have the receipt? I don't think so – unless you're really heartless. Seriously, how many policies and procedures have been enforced on you (or by you) that you would never enforce on someone you care about? Probably dozens, if not hundreds.

As you read the four core beliefs that I generated from my list of caring attributes, you may have noticed that each caring attribute was not specifically represented, and yet they all have a voice in my core beliefs. Whether I'm doing a presentation to hundreds of people, consulting on an individual basis, or simply returning a phone call, these core beliefs are always the driving force behind everything I do. Now it's your turn to translate your list of caring attributes into your list of business core beliefs. Go ahead - get to work!

Your policies and procedures will often have very little to do with your business' success, but your core beliefs will have everything to do with it.

This is critical. Take your time and think through this process. I've provided space for five core beliefs, but please don't be limited by my numbering system. This is way too important. My only suggestion is don't create too many core beliefs. It's better to have just a few that are strong, so their message is clear and understandable.

My Core Beliefs of Service

1. ————————————————————————————

2. ————————————————————————————

3. ————————————————————————————

4. ————————————————————————————

5. ————————————————————————————

If you've completed composing your list of core beliefs, that's great because you can't leave them locked up in that steel-trap brain of yours. They must be written down to bring them to life. Get them on paper and turn your thoughts into something tangible. Once they're written down, keep them on your desk, hang them on a wall, and share them with your employees at every opportunity. After all, these core beliefs are not a part of your company – they *are* your company. When you consistently translate these words into actions, the belief will truly set in.

One point of note. Essential #1, Creating your Vision, is unique in that your vision must be completed before moving on to the other essentials. The remaining disciplines may be planned, initiated and evaluated as you work through the process. But your core beliefs must be solid. Taking your core beliefs a step further, your business' mission statement should clearly reflect your core beliefs amidst the explanation of why your business exists.

Over time, you may have to make adjustments to your vision as customer needs and wants change, or as your business adapts to variations in the market. But your vision is designed to be the cornerstone and cannot be something that continually changes. It must have integrity to survive. If it is shaky or unclear, developing a *Service with Purpose* culture will be nearly impossible.

What's my point? DO NOT move on without having a vision and core beliefs that you truly believe in. If you do honestly believe in your vision and your core beliefs, you're ready to roll.

Your Imaginary Grocery Store

As you design your vision, make sure you raise the bar high enough to challenge yourself and your business. Greatness was never achieved by being mediocre, so don't set mediocre goals for yourself. How do I define mediocre? It may not be the way you define it. Consider these two scenarios...

We've all been to a grocery store and have a pretty good idea of how a usual visit should proceed. So let's stop in at Joe's Grocery Store now. As you read, look for the points of customer contact and evaluate how Joe's Grocery Store is doing.

The sky is blue. It is a beautiful day. You find a parking space not far from the entrance of Joe's Grocery Store. You enter the store and find it to be clean and well lit. The aisles are well marked and the shelves are full of the products you're looking for. You're happy that your shopping cart's wheels don't make that annoying squeaking sound as you push it throughout the store.

At the deli counter, you take a number and are waited on in a timely fashion. The butcher smiles as he weighs your cold cuts.

When you've finished your shopping, you walk to the front of the store and find several cashiers quickly ringing up the shoppers ahead of you. After you load all of your purchases on the conveyer, the cashier rings them up and a bagger loads them back into your cart. You pay the cashier and as you walk away, she smiles and says, "Thank you. Have a nice day."

What do you think? Was it great service or simply mediocre? I suppose that would depend on what sort of expectations you had. Years of experiencing bad service may have lowered your expectations. If you're like many consumers, being able to visit a store and buy what you want with no one being rude, without being ignored, and in general having nothing bad happen makes it a great place to shop. But wouldn't you agree that a consumer should be able to walk into any retail establishment and find courteous employees, great product selection and a positive shopping environment? Of course you would. And when your expectations are met, you're satisfied. You're content.

The lack of a negative service experience does not necessarily mean it was a positive experience.

With all that being said, if you simply had average expectations, is there anything that happened at Joe's Grocery Store that would be above average? Probably not. But exceeding customer expectations is what *Service with Purpose* is all about.

Joe's Grocery Store doesn't provide bad service; in fact, they're "not bad." They meet your expectations of what a visit to a grocery store should be. When you consistently *meet* your customers expectations, you become a provider of average customer service and you receive good "customer satisfaction" ratings. Your customers say stuff like, "Yeah, they're pretty good. Not bad."

That's not what we're looking for. It is the goal of every *Service with Purpose* business to exceed expectations at every possible opportunity.

So let's see what can you do. Suppose you open your own grocery store and Joe's Grocery Store is right down the road from you. What can you do? Think about this for a second. While Joe's certainly didn't fail on any level and everything that happened was basically positive, how could you exceed customer expectations?

If you don't mind, I'm going to visit your store. Yes, you do own a grocery store and it's a place where expectations are exceeded and service magic happens on a daily basis. Boy, I can hardly wait!

As I pull in to your parking lot, I notice that you have free valet parking so I take advantage of the service. I'm given a number to retrieve my car when I've finished my shopping.

As I enter your store, a young woman – who serves as the stores greeter – hands me a flyer that highlights all of today's specials and has a small map of the store. She also invites me to take a free cup of coffee, tea or a soft drink. And hey, look at this: my cart has a cup holder built right in! Wow, not bad!

"If you have children with you today," the greeter says, "make sure you take them to our supervised Playland area. Your kids will love it!"

I thank her and enthusiastically make my way into your store. The air is filled with the aroma of delicious foods. Sample stands are located throughout the store – and not with just your typical meat on a toothpick. These samples were prepared using various items sold in the store to show creative new recipes and food preparation techniques. As I make my way through the store, I actually find myself beginning to feel full from eating so many of the wonderful samples.

When I've completed my shopping and make my way to the checkout line, I'm stopped by a checkout agent who suggests that since there is a line she'll take my cart and total all of my groceries for me. She also requests to have my valet parking ticket. In the meantime, she directs me to the Guest Lounge where I can wait until my groceries are totaled.

The Guest Lounge is clean, bright and well maintained. Big, comfortable chairs surround several TVs tuned to various channels. Current magazines and newspapers are plentiful. Again, free coffee and soft drinks are available. After only a few short minutes, I hear my name called over the public address system. I approach the checkout counter and pay for my groceries. "Your car is waiting for you right outside."

As I exit the store, I walk towards my waiting car, which is already loaded with my groceries. A young man working as the valet asks to see my receipt. "There you go, sir. Your car is all loaded up and ready to go. By the way, sir, if you use our valet parking next Saturday, we will be providing free car washes to all of our store guests."

How about that? Is there any question as to what kind of service this was? Is there any question as to whether or not I will be telling everyone I know about the incredible experience I had at your grocery store? Is there any question at all as to whether or not you've exceeded my expectations? Of course you did! Great job! By the way, you really nailed your points of customer contact.

Now, think back to our experience at Joe's Grocery Store. Before we visited your grocery store, the service you received at Joe's seemed pretty good. Joe's basically provided what you would expect from a good store: clean, fast, quality, friendly. You know, the basics.

But at your grocery store, you've exceeded my expectations at every turn. At every moment you reminded me that this wasn't just any ol' grocery store. When that happens, you've created the magic that will forever separate you from the Joe's Groceries of the world.

What would be some examples of the core beliefs that are undoubtedly taught and practiced at your grocery store? What do you think? Well, you should know since it is your grocery store. But if you've forgotten, I did get a peek inside your manual and read a few of your core beliefs.

They read something like this…

Core Belief #1

"The food items in our store will not be presented as mere commodities. The customers at our store will be able to experience the tastes, smells, creative uses and presentations of the products we offer."

Core Belief #2

"When it comes to our customers, they will be treated like respected members of our family. We will go out of our way to surprise our customers with the amount of attention and assistance we provide to them on every visit."

Core Belief #3

If a customer approaches us with a question, a request or a complaint, we will take ownership of the problem and see it through to the customer's delight."

These are pretty powerful beliefs. Strong beliefs build strong foundations where a service culture can flourish.

All This Sounds Great, but...

Everything sounds wonderful in the previous grocery store scenario. But what if you're only a spoke in the wheel, a front-liner or in middle management and you don't have the authority to make those radical types of changes? Maybe the company's service vision has already been thought out for you. Or maybe your company doesn't have any idea of what a service vision is. Well then, you've got your hands full, but there is an answer.

You know things could be better, but what can you do? The first thing is to take note of the things that could be done better and visualize them the way you would like them to be. If parts of your vision include major changes, take time to think them through and then make a suggestion to the people who can make it happen. If you feel strongly enough, you could even make a formal presentation to your manager. However you present your ideas, be sure to offer solutions and the benefits they will provide. Don't get yourself in the position where you are only pointing out everything that is wrong. If you do this, you can be viewed as a complainer – and nobody wants that.

When there is an area where you can make the change yourself, do it. Take inventory of what you can control. If there are things happening in your company that you perceive to be negative but you simply cannot control or change them, decide how best to work around those obstacles. Change what you can change; accept what you cannot. Visualize your service culture and do the best you can with what you have.

Remember, the only way to achieve great results is to set high goals and high standards. Many companies can achieve moderate success without a strong commitment to service. But at the saying goes, "You don't fall to the top of the mountain." Within your realm of control, be sure to set service goals that will challenge you and your organization, and you'll be off and running.

"Vision is knowing who you are, where you're going and what will guide your journey."

– From *Full Steam Ahead*
Ken Blanchard & Jesse Stoner

The Six Essentials of Service

1 - Vision

2 - Hiring

3 -

4 -

5 -

6 -

Chapter 11:

Essential #2

Hiring

"You can dream, create, design and build the most wonderful place in the world...
But it requires people to make the dream a reality.
– Walt Disney

The people who work for your company *are* your company. No matter how strongly you believe in your vision, if the people around you don't support the vision, it will never become a reality.

I don't think I can be any clearer than that. To create a *Service with Purpose* business, you cannot do it alone. You can be the driving force, but true service success can only be achieved by the individuals that make up the team.

By hiring the right people from the beginning, you will give yourself the best chance of fulfilling your vision.

"The greatest things are accomplished by individual people, not by committees or companies."

-Alfred A. Montapert

This *Service with Purpose* philosophy can operate in just about any kind of business. But one of the areas that seems to give employers the most challenges year after year is hiring front-line employees. From cashiers to waiters and waitresses to desk clerks, often your potential labor pool is comprised of teenagers or part-time employees vying for minimum wage positions and bringing little experience with them.

If your labor pool includes professionals or other higher paying positions, your job is still the same. You must determine if the applicants are diamonds in the rough, or just rough. The ability to uncover their value is critical to hiring wisely. When you hire wisely, you add a new talent, a new personality to your business that will help you live up to your core beliefs and improve your business. To have any hope of uncovering this hidden treasure in the form of a new employee, you must start by being prepared for the interview.

Before you ever hang the "Now Hiring" sign on your front window, know what kind of attributes you're looking for in your employees. Which attributes are most important in helping you achieve your vision? Which personality traits will work best with your core beliefs?

Do you need people who smile a lot? Then don't ever hire someone who stares blankly at you as he answers your interview questions. Do you need employees with integrity, enthusiasm, experience or a great attitude? You'd probably like all of those things. To find people like this, you must observe and ask questions about things that will reveal this information.

In most situations, first look for the personality traits you desire first. Then consider their experience. It is much easier to teach someone a new skill, than to create a new personality or attitude. Generally speaking, if you start by hiring people with good attitudes, you're probably on the right track. Find employees who have the potential to care about their work, because employees must care above all else.

Now don't get lazy just because you've hired someone with the right attitude. His or her attitude will decline if it is not nurtured. You can't just expect to say, "Okay everybody, start caring!" You must create a *culture* of service and caring. Creating a service culture is a tall order, but the Six Essentials of Service, all working together, is the way to achieve it. Initially finding people that are capable of caring, with good attitudes and a positive outlook, will give you a good start.

If you do have the opportunity to control who gets hired, here are three key tips for your hiring success:

Three Keys for Hiring Potential Stars
(Particularly for front-line employees.)

1. Do your homework.

Call references. Research suggests that the best way employers can accurately predict an employee's future behavior is by looking at his past behavior under similar circumstances. Has the applicant been a shining star in the past, or does he have a "checkered" past?

Review the application or résumé closely. How's the spelling and grammar? You would hope an applicant would do their best work on an application in hopes of getting an interview. If the application is sloppy or incomplete, you may have all the information you'll need to make a decision on that person.

2. Learn how to interview well.

This obviously is easier said than done. But it's worth taking the time to learn the necessary skills to be a master interviewer. You can start by developing a good list of interview questions.

Again, know what attributes you're looking for and develop questions to identify them. For example, if you're looking for someone who is outgoing, "how soon can you start?" may not be a good opening question.

A great way to learn about your applicant is by asking open-ended questions. These would be questions that cannot be answered with a simple "yes" or "no." The applicant must be able to think and respond. While the ability to think and respond intelligently seems to be somewhat rare in the service industry, you're here to change all of that.

Don't be afraid to ask questions that put your applicants on the spot. Doing this may reveal some insight into the applicant's thought processes and his or her ability to handle stress. For example, ask a hypothetical question like, "If you were getting ready to close and a customer entered the store and wanted you to remain open for an extra 20 minutes so she could browse, what would you do?" The answers to this question could be very interesting. How would your existing employees answer this question? How would you answer it? Would all of your current employees answer it the same way? Would they answer it the way you'd like it to be answered?

If you want to be really tricky, there's a great follow-up question that isn't used nearly often enough. This type of question is used repeatedly and with great professionalism by four-year-olds all around the world. The question is "Why?" or "What?" or any other question that forces the applicant to dig a little deeper and justify or explain her first response. This works well because if the applicant prepared for the interview at all, she most likely prepared answers for expected questions. But applicants almost never plan for second or third responses to the same questions.

If the applicant didn't prepare at all, it's a good opportunity to see if she has the ability to think on her feet. Honestly, it's also slightly enjoyable to watch applicants squirm a little.

When your applicant answers an open-ended question, follow up with another question. For example, "Susan, you said that you applied with our company because you enjoy working with the public. What are some of the aspects of dealing with the public that you enjoy?"

The second question is valuable because just about anyone can spit out, "I like dealing with the public." But for the most part only someone who truly feels that way can produce convincing reasons to support his statement right on the spot.

3. Listen more than you talk.

When you've taken the time to develop and pose thought-provoking questions, make sure you remember to stop talking and let your applicant respond. Again, if you're looking for an outgoing employee and he appears to be introverted and reluctant when answering your questions, you may not have a match. Even if the person seems kind and considerate, if you're looking for outgoing, stick to your guns and hold out for someone who is more of an extrovert. Whatever characteristics you're looking for, make sure you give the applicant ample talking time so you can make a strong determination.

It's extremely important to bring the right people into your organization and an incredibly expensive mistake to bring in the wrong ones. Be creative with your interviews to find the people you need.

There's no question that at times you'll begin to wonder if there are any diamonds in the rough left out there. They *are* out there; you just need to keep looking. If you find the pool of applicants to be too "shallow" to find the right people, expand your search. If you're not receiving enough applicants by advertising the positions the old way (whatever that is), try new approaches to finding the people you need. Eventually, word-of-mouth advertising will be your most powerful "Help Wanted" sign. By creating an inviting workplace, you will have more and more people wanting to work for you, and it will become easier for you to become more selective in the hiring process.

Working with Existing Employees

In addition to hiring new people, you will also have to deal with existing employees. Change can be difficult for everyone at times. When introducing new ideas or programs, remember to be patient and give your existing employees a lot of support and encouragement. Let them see your commitment. As the saying goes, "Your actions speak so loudly, I cannot hear what you say."

Creating a customer-focused business is a team effort. At times no matter what you do, you'll encounter employees who either refuse or are incapable of adjusting to your service vision. After giving them ample support, training and feedback, if no improvement is seen, unfortunately they will have to be let go. It can be difficult at times. But if your vision is created around service and someone isn't responding to that kind of environment, maybe they're just not the right kind of person for that job. It doesn't mean that these are bad people; it simply means that they may not be suited to work within the parameters of your vision. Misguided loyalty to an uncommitted employee can truly be disastrous for everyone – including the employee.

On the positive side, once your employees are hired, you want to keep them and keep them happy. The way to do this is to establish a strong training program. That's why the third essential in the process is training. A strong training program, which includes an orientation program, will reduce stress, boost job satisfaction and help new employees become productive more quickly.

Do what you can do. When others see that you're not just some crazy gung-ho butt-kisser, but someone who is truly doing his best for himself and his company, others will soon begin to follow your lead.

Note to front-liners and middle managers: If you cannot pick and choose your co-workers, make the best of what you've got. Share your ideas for making things better. Always maintain a high level of enthusiasm. Most importantly, let your co-workers see your actions.

The Six Essentials of Service

1 - Vision

2 - Hiring

3 - Training

4 -

5 -

6 -

Chapter 12:

Essential #3

Training

Although each of the disciplines required to create the *Service with Purpose* business are non-negotiable, the training step is definitely the driving force. Training provides the momentum, the confidence and most importantly, the belief your employees will need to create a caring service culture.

Training provides the fuel that keeps your employees moving forward and maintaining interest in their responsibilities. Without training, apathy soon sets in; your new employees never achieve their potential and eventually quit. Or worse yet, your employees quit but never tell you about it. They just keep showing up for work, doing as little as possible and collecting their paychecks. Unfortunately, this is probably the status of many workers in the service industry today. Training alone will not fully solve this problem, but a lack of training will definitely cause it, or make it worse.

"No problem," you say, "We train all of our new hires right before they start working for us." Well, maybe you do have it covered, but the training that creates the type of service magic you want isn't a one-shot deal like most introductory training sessions. You know the ones; you've probably sat (or slept) through a few of them yourself. If you were sleeping, hopefully you weren't the one conducting the session.

Anyway, you know how the sessions go, "Welcome to our great company. Here's your uniform. There's where you punch in. Do this. Don't do that. Blah. Blah. Blah." I don't mean to say that the less exciting aspects of a new job are not important for new hires to learn. But many – make that most – businesses provide training sessions just like this, then they never follow up or hold another training session or provide any feedback until the next batch of new hires arrives. And they think they've fully prepared their new employees to succeed.

If you're providing this kind of training - at least you're trying. But the type of training provided by world-class companies is not only thorough, it's also never-ending. Additionally, beyond just the "who's," "what's," "when's" and "where's," of most introductory training sessions, your training must plant the seeds of your company's culture. This would be the "why."

> If your employees don't know *why* they do what they do, nothing else matters.

Your training will explain to your new employees why your company does what it does and how they fit into the big picture of what you do. Kristin Accipiter, a spokeswoman for the Society for Human Resource Management, said, "Successful companies have made orientation more like (a family) adoption than a two-hour, one-sided lecture." She goes on to say that these companies "treat employees as if they were family members." What better way to help new employees embrace your service vision than to treat them like family and make them feel in the loop?

Another great way to get new employees to start internalizing your service vision is to have each employee write himself or herself a letter from a fictitious customer that highlights three aspects of the employee's behavior, attitude or skills that made a positive impact on the customer's experience with your business. Then share these letters with the group. It will be amazing how the items written by the fictitious customer will start becoming a reality.

With all this in mind, remember that there is no end to training. To be effective, your training must be consistent, thorough and never-ending. Period.

Almost as famous (or infamous) as the one-and-ready introductory training sessions are the classic "Smile Training" sessions. You know, the ones that suggest you keep a mirror at your desk to make sure that you're smiling while you're on the phone so your voice sounds happy. Of course if you hate your job, hate your customers, and – dare I say – hate your boss, that fake smile isn't going to be too convincing.

Smile Training tries to solve the problem by working on the symptoms, not the cause. Wouldn't it be nice if your employees smiled because they were happy and not because they were continually instructed to do so? The companies that put service at the top of their priority list do provide their employees with the skills necessary to deliver outstanding service. But they also work to make sure their employees have the positive attitudes to go along with their skills. It takes both skill and attitude to bring service to life.

> *"The best morale exists when you never hear the word mentioned. When you hear a lot of talk about it, it's usually lousy."*
>
> -Dwight D. Eisenhower

If you do hold Smile Training – by this name or any other – I have two questions for you. First, why would you hire someone who doesn't already know how to smile or be nice? Secondly, do you honestly think you can tell someone to smile and be nice if they really don't want to? Smiles only come from people who are happy to be doing what they're doing. Don't believe me? Have you ever been told to "have a nice day" by someone who really didn't care if you had a good day or not? Maybe it was just something they had to say and they even mustered up the energy to crack a smile. Didn't it really just make you feel really special inside?

If you currently have no training program, now is the time to start one. But where do you begin? Start with the core beliefs that you decided would be the foundation of your business or department. Find ways to share those thoughts with your employees.

But be warned: whatever you do, make sure you're walking the walk before you start talking the talk. What I mean by this is don't write your core beliefs down on fancy parchment and pass them out or display them on a plaque without supporting them with action. Make sure that you're prepared to *live* your core beliefs before you start telling others how important they are. Your core beliefs need to be seen in the way you treat your employees, your customers, your policies, your training. Remember, your words are worthless if there isn't consistent, strong action to back them up. If you're not living it, don't even say it.

Extensive research shows that well-planned training programs for new employees will reduce their stress levels, boost job satisfaction and help new employees become productive more quickly.

Sam Walton, the founder of Wal-Mart, once said that it takes just seven days for new employees to start treating customers the way they themselves are treated at work. Don't put off bringing your employees into the loop. Make them a part of the team as soon as possible. Get them into that introductory training and into your business' culture, preferably before they ever work a shift.

The trick is not to stop there. Keep training, cross training, evaluating. And, remember, no matter how much training you do, employees will learn what is acceptable by watching what those who have higher positions say and (most importantly) do.

What type of training should I use?

Training can take many forms: classroom instruction, videos, role-playing, manuals, seminars, audio programs, mentoring, observation, and more. The best training programs include many different techniques and approaches. Yours should too.

Experiment with different approaches and choose the method of training that is practical and best suited for your needs. If you're not sure what type of training to use, here are a few facts to think about.

- We retain 20% of what we hear.
- We retain 30% of what we see.
- We retain 70% of what we say.
- We retain 90% of what we say and do.

The last point suggests that if your employees will be interacting with customers, put them in situations that simulate customer contact, like role playing. Simply lecturing employees on what to say in different situations can be informative, but having your employees practice what is actually going to be required of them can be much more productive.

Obviously, there is a financial cost associated with training; but instead of viewing training as an expense, consider it to be an investment. Of course, everyone's situation is different, but here is a starting point. Tom Connellan, author of *Inside the Magic Kingdom*, reports that for every $100 in financial compensation, world-class companies invest $5-6 in training. So if a new employee is going to be earning $20,000 a year, you should be investing approximately $1,100 to train her. Sound expensive? Maybe not when you compare it to the following statistics.

According to a study done by the management consulting firm, Sibson & Company, the costs of replacing an employee at even an entry-level position can be staggering.

Assuming a profit margin of 10%, to recoup the cost of losing just one sales clerk, a clothing store must sell almost 3,000 pairs of khakis at $35 each.

Assuming a profit margin of 8%, to recoup the cost of losing just one employee, a fast food restaurant must sell 7,613 children's combo meals at $2.50 each.

Solid training will help reduce turnover. If you haven't figured it out yet, the point of this story is that high turnover is very costly. According to the Sibson & Company study, in industries where turnover is common – like specialty retailing and fast food – high turnover can reduce earnings and stock prices by an average of 38%.

High turnover in these or other industries not only creates a financial burden to replace employees, it also impacts a company's ability to keep current customers, attract new ones, increase productivity or pursue growth opportunities.

Making Your Training Work

You may be thinking to yourself, "I'm doing the training but I'm just not getting the results I'm hoping for." There could be many reasons why your training efforts are not paying off. Maybe you're using the wrong approach; maybe it's not consistent with your core beliefs.

Consider this example of a family-owned bowling center. This neighborhood bowling center took pride in being a clean, safe place where people would come to relax and have fun. An outstanding source of revenue for this bowling center was children's birthday parties. Unfortunately, every year they were holding fewer and fewer parties. The bowling center was committed to making their birthday party business profitable and providing an outstanding event for each of their customers. But despite their best efforts, the numbers declined year after year.

The very wise owner of the bowling center decided to buy a copy of *Who Cares?*, read it and apply its principles. (Yeah, that was blatant self-promotion.) The owner called a meeting with his managers and his best birthday party hosts and hostesses to review the company's core beliefs and to try and correct their sagging party business. After brainstorming for a while, the owner asked his managers what single element was more important than any other for a successful birthday party. Each attendee answered without a doubt that their guests having fun was more important than any aspect of the outing. Since the intentions of every birthday party should be to have fun, they were probably correct.

With this information in mind, they reviewed the training material they used for their new birthday party hosts and hostesses. Their training material was incredibly elaborate. From beginning to end, every detail was listed, including how to greet, how to help the children select the correct shoes and bowling balls, when to serve the food, when to sing "Happy Birthday," when to clean up – it was all there. Everything down to the smallest detail was painstakingly listed for the new employees.

But there was one thing that was strikingly absent from their training material. Well it was almost absent. There in the last paragraph of the very last page of their training manual were two short sentences that read, "Birthday parties are intended to be fun. It's okay for you to have fun at work." This was the only place in their entire training program that even included the word "fun." Keep in mind, fun was said to be the most important part of a party, and yet it was only mentioned in passing.

They immediately began to address the problem. Up to this point, their party hosts and hostesses had been efficient and knew all of the rules, but there was something missing. They had never been instilled with the company's vision and core beliefs. In other words, they had never connected the "why" with the "how."

When the bowling center changed their training to be more fun-centered than procedurally centered, the transformation had begun. The new training focused on many new ideas including games that could be played with the children, jokes and funny stories that could be shared, and even a few simple magic tricks. They were determined to exceed their customers' expectations. And the party hosts and hostesses were evaluated and rewarded based on how well they achieved their goals, both individually and as a team.

Within months, the positive word-of-mouth advertising generated from their new and improved birthdays had their party revenue on the rise for the first time in years. It all changed because they started educating their own people on what their company stood for.

The moral of the story is to keep your training in line with your core beliefs.

Help your employees to understand your core beliefs and how to make them real for your customers.

Watch Out for Conflicting Priorities

Make sure your training doesn't unintentionally confuse your employees and "muddy" your message. It can sometimes be very easy to create goals for your employees that conflict with one another. Let's say one of your core beliefs involves serving each customer in a timely manner and another core belief extols the virtues of always going the extra mile for every customer. Both of these core beliefs are very commendable and worthwhile – but watch how your set up your practical actions, procedures and reward programs. They may be working against each other.

Encouraging employees to achieve conflicting goals is a common problem and a typical cause for employee complaints. For example, to encourage speedy service you've set up a reward program that recognizes employees who can wait on at least ten customers every thirty minutes. For this, they are rewarded with a certificate at the monthly employee meeting. You're feeling pretty good now because you know that your employees are trying to meet at least one of your core beliefs – in this case, timely service.

But then there's Annie, an average employee in your mind. She shows up for work, doesn't complain, and has a good attitude, but she's just so darn slow. She's the slowest worker you've got. You've even thought about disciplining her a time or two. "But she's a nice girl," you think to yourself. "She won't amount to much working here, but at least she's trying."

What's the problem here? Two things. First, if you ever find yourself disappointed with an employee's performance, let them know. You owe that to them, and it's the only way they can improve. We'll talk more about providing feedback to employees in an upcoming chapter.

The second problem is that when Annie went to her introductory training session and had the company's core beliefs explained to her, the one core belief that struck a cord with Annie was how everyone who works for your company should always go the extra mile for your customers. With Annie being the people person she is, she thought this was just a great concept and embraced this belief from her very first day of work. She regularly stops to answer customers' questions and explain things they don't understand. She always tries to make a personal connection with her customers by making conversation and showing a sincere interest in them. She's even left her register for a moment or two to show a customer where something was located in the store that they couldn't find on their own.

And yet, despite her best efforts in trying to achieve the company's core beliefs (at least from her point of view), she was never recognized at any monthly employee meeting or ever given so much as a "Good Job." It turns out that you, the manager, were only recognizing and rewarding one of your core beliefs – timely service.

Annie, on the other hand, was also only working on one of your core beliefs, just not the same one that you were paying attention to.

What do you think happened to Annie's attitude? When she gets fed up and quits (or you fire her), what type of complaints would she make about working for you or your company? Would these be justified? Make sure your goals and rewards work in unity.

"You get what you reward."

-Ken Blanchard

Dealing with Upset Customers

Through the development of your vision and procedures and policies, your focus has been and will continue to be – the prevention of problems with your procedures and people. It's the old adage: "An ounce of prevention is worth a pound of cure." While that holds true, sometimes no matter what you do, you're going to have people get upset with you, your procedures, policies or your employees.

Avoid customer problems by teaching your employees to start with "Yes." Don't waste time making excuses to try to explain what you can't or are not willing to do. Tell your customers what you *can* do to help them.

How you train your employees to deal with these situations can mean the difference between retaining your hard-earned customers or having to go out and "buy" some new ones with advertising or other promotional tactics. Service Recovery is the art of resolving a customer's problem to his satisfaction. Research suggests that when complaints are resolved quickly, up to 95 percent of the customers will do business with the company again. In fact, a customer who has had a negative situation resolved quickly and satisfactorily may become even more loyal than a customer who has never encountered a negative situation with your business. Point being, it's not necessarily what happened that is important; it's what you do about it that matters.

Here's a short "to do" list when dealing with upset customers.

1. Teach employees to take all complaints seriously.

Whether the complaint seems ridiculous to you or not, your customer believes it is important enough to report it. That in itself should make it important to you as well.

2. Listen closely to the complaint.

Don't respond until you've had a chance to hear everything the customer has to say.

3. Ask the customer what they'd like you to do.

This may be the most powerful question of all. My experience has been that when you ask a customer how they'd like a situation to be resolved, they usually ask for less than you were prepared to give them. But the idea here is that you cared enough about their complaint to give them control over their own situation.

4. Empathize with the customer.

Saying things like, "I can see how this would upset you," doesn't mean that the customer is right and you're wrong. It simply means that you listened to them and can sincerely appreciate their feelings. Sometimes this is all the customer was looking for.

Sometimes, the complaining customer is actually wrong. But it doesn't matter. The customer may not always be right, but they are always the customer. Making a disgruntled customer happy is often less expensive than finding a new one.

5. Take ownership of the problem.

Have you ever heard any of these statements?

"I'm sorry, that's not my department. You'll have to hang up and call us back on another number."

"Your warranty just expired. There's nothing I can do… You'll have to contact the manufacturer."

"I can't help you with that. You'll have to speak with my manager, and he's not available right now."

These statements undoubtedly would infuriate you. Don't allow them to happen at your business. Author and consultant Jeffrey Gitomer says, "Own the problem, own the customer. Lose the problem, lose the customer."

6. Resolve the situation.

Teach your employees how to resolve as many types of problems as possible. This involves giving your employees the ability and authority to resolve problems. This power you bestow upon your employees is called *empowerment*.

Energy Killer – Avoid making a bad situation worse. Don't put your customers on the defensive by blaming them for the situation or saying things like… "Calm down" or "What's your problem?"

Emotion vs. Logic

Understanding the thought processes of your customers can be a valuable tool when trying to resolve a negative situation. Often an upset customer can seem like nothing more than a crazy person who won't get off the phone or out of your face. Frankly, sometimes they may be crazy people, but that's another story. For our example, let's assume they're just really upset and not crazy.

How did the customer get worked into this frenzy? How did he go from a quiet, happy customer to a ranting nuisance? This transformation most likely didn't happen instantaneously. The odds are that a person, procedure or policy in your company had something to do with the situation.

Although we like to believe otherwise, human beings are predominantly emotional creatures. When we're at our favorite restaurant, we say we "like the attentive service," but what we really mean is that "the waiter makes us feel important during our entire meal." Loyal customers are built on emotional connections, not logical ones. If logic always won, the store with the lowest prices would always win, and that's not the case.

Bernice Johnston, author of *Real World Customer Service*, states that there are three levels of "emotional escalation": Disappointment, Frustration and Anger. When a problem arises for a customer, his first reaction is typically disappointment. At this point, if you resolve the problem quickly, there's practically no harm done and the customer is very appreciative. If the problem is not resolved quickly, the customer moves from disappointment to frustration.

"Why does the cashier keep staring at me like I'm crazy?"

"Why do they keep putting me on hold?"

"Why do they keep transferring me from department to department?"

"Why do they keep telling me about their policies? I don't care!"

The customer's ability to be rational and to apply logic begins to diminish as her negative emotional energy begins to build up until it finally explodes from frustration to full-blown anger.

When the anger phase hits, logic is out the window. "You're a jerk." "Your company stinks." "You're a bunch of idiots." "I wouldn't buy anything from you if you were the last business on Earth!" Lots of emotion – very little logic. Now, even if you eventually resolve this situation for the customer, you've got some serious fence mending to do. Don't force a customer to get angry if you're eventually going to do what he wants anyway.

Resolve problems quickly and turn a customer's disappointment into a pleasant surprise that will pay dividends far into the future.

Empower Your Employees

Do you know what is the biggest problem with most employee manuals and policies? Company manuals and policies are most often written to explain to your employees what they or your customers *cannot* do. It is written from the company's point of view, often for the company's "protection." Most manuals are written with the sole purpose of looking out for – only caring about – the company. Can you see the problem this may cause for a company that is supposed to care about their customers like family?

Now that you have a new perspective on things, make sure your policies are customer centered. Let your employees know what they *can* do for their customers instead of only what they can't. For example, many great service-minded companies allow all of their employees to spend a predetermined amount of money on a customer to make them happy. No questions asked. Taking care of the customer is the priority.

This brings up a good point, do your employees know what they can do to make your customers happy and solve their problems? Are they authorized to do whatever it takes, or do they have to receive permission in order to do anything?

Having your employees know what they can do to make your customers happy is far more important than knowing what they cannot do.

When you give your employees the ability to make decisions on their own, they become "empowered." Empowerment is critical for service success. Although most businesses can see the value of having empowered employees, very few embrace it in a meaningful way. And yet, those companies that do effectively embrace empowerment are legendary service providers.

"Let the inmates run the asylum? Are you crazy?" Business managers and owners are often quite defensive about this issue. The prevailing thought is that employees either aren't smart enough or can't be trusted to make decisions of this nature. Beyond that, it's generally believed that the customer will always take advantage of the situation. Ask yourself this: Is the sale of a $5 lunch more important than the value of a happy, loyal customer? The answer is obvious, and yet businesses continue to hold on to their pennies instead of satisfying their customers.

Let me give you an example of a situation I encountered where the employees were either not trained to be empowered or they weren't permitted or encouraged to think on their own.

Sorry, There's No Room at the Inn

Our family had planned our annual trip to a large theme park and we booked a room for the weekend at one of the park's hotels. This hotel was special to me because it was the hotel my parents used to take me to when I was a kid. I have a lot of great memories from my youth and wanted to share those experiences with my wife and children.

I knew we'd be arriving at the hotel late in the evening based on our travel time, so I called the hotel at 6 PM to verify our reservation.

"I just wanted to let you know that we will be arriving tonight even though it might be a little late," I started. "I know when hotels are busy they tend to over book and I want to make sure we'll have a room when we get there."

"Yes, Mr. Brown," the voice on the other end said. "We have your reservation and we'll be expecting you. Thanks for calling to confirm your arrival."

It was a brief but productive phone conversation, and I felt quite good about myself having had the foresight to be that organized. Being the typical man that I am, I even made sure to mention my organizational skills to my wife.

It was just about midnight when we pulled into the hotel parking lot. My kids were asleep in the car and my wife was barely awake. I left the car running and entered the hotel. There were three people working at the desk when I announced, "My name is Scott Brown and I'm here to check in." At that, two of the people who were behind the counter suddenly walked away. Apparently, they had forgotten to do something very important based on their haste in exiting the scene.

The lone remaining desk clerk kept her eyes focused on her computer screen without ever looking up at me. "I'm sorry, Mr. Brown. We're unfortunately booked this evening. If you'd like, we'd be happy to put you up a the "Cheapo Lodge" across the street for free this evening, and then you can check in here after 11 AM tomorrow." (It wasn't really called the "Cheapo Lodge," but you get the point.)

"Well, I figured you were going to be sold out this evening. That's why I called to make sure I would have a room waiting when we arrived. You should probably check the reservation again," I said with some confidence.

That didn't seem to help. She refused to look at me and kept telling me how lucky I was to be getting a free night of lodging. When I continued to press the issue, I could see her cheeks getting red and she asked me to stop yelling at her. She actually said that. You'll have to take my word for this, but I don't yell, get obnoxious, nasty or rude. She simply didn't like the fact that I wouldn't let this drop. I wanted a positive resolution. I didn't create this problem. They did!

Maybe if I hadn't called ahead I would have responded differently. But I did call ahead, and dragging my luggage from one hotel to another over a short weekend was not worth a free room. Not to mention the fact that my wife would be chewing my ear off for the rest of the trip. Basically, all I wanted was the desk clerk to admit that their basic guest blow-off procedure was very wrong – especially in my case. Well, when I walked out of that lobby 45 minutes later, all I had achieved was a free breakfast buffet for my family and the name of the morning manager.

So I found myself unloading my car in the middle of the night and hauling my bags up two flights of stairs at the Cheapo Lodge, sleeping for a few hours, repacking my suitcases, and reloading my car early the next morning. After that pleasant experience, I headed back to our originally scheduled hotel. I approached the reservation desk and asked for the manager. He arrived in a timely manner and I explained the situation to him. He said, "You're right. That shouldn't have happened." (That's all I wanted the desk clerk to say the previous night, but she just wouldn't do it!) Then he asked what, in my opinion, is the magic question when dealing with an upset customer: "What can I do to make it better for you?" He put the resolution of the situation in my hands.

Without waiting for me to answer his question, the manager asked if a free night at his hotel would be satisfactory. I quickly agreed to his suggestion. This was agreeable to me not only because I wound up saving a lot of money, but because he listened to what I had to say and responded based on the situation, not the manual. And not to be overlooked, while a free night's lodging has a great perceived value, the cost of this gesture on the part of the hotel was minimal – especially if they had rooms available. Regardless, this seems like a small price to pay to keep a good customer.

The desk clerk from the night before looked at me as being hostile because I wasn't playing by their rules. I became her nemesis, her enemy, and the one who makes her job stressful… No, I wasn't. I just needed her to be on my side. I was right and they were wrong – period. She knew that, but she wouldn't admit it.

Maybe she didn't have the authority. Maybe she didn't know any better. Regardless, before this desk clerk stood a customer whose family had spent thousands of dollars at this resort over the years, and she refused to even look me in the eye.

The manager resolved the situation for me and I will return to this hotel. But they nearly lost a good customer and caused tremendous frustration for everyone involved. It didn't have to be that way.

If the desk clerk had been trained to be a problem-solver instead of a problem "dealer wither," she might have been able to help me. That's what most people who work on the front lines are, you know – "dealer withers." If there's a problem with a customer, a manager expects the front-liner to "deal with it."

"If the customer gets rude or more angry, then call me," managers often say. At that point, the manager will decide if the customer should get their money back, can return the product, or maybe he'll even find a room for them in the hotel they're supposed to be staying in. That would be nice for a change.

But more often than not, many companies have the incredibly insightful, unwritten policy that reads something like this...

"Note to front-liners: Your job is to make sure the customers follow our rules. Our rules are one size fits all. If they don't fit... it doesn't matter. Make them fit. If for some reason this does not satisfy the customer, then call me, your manager, and I'll deal with the jerk. Sometimes – just like you – I'll make our rules fit – even if it makes our customer even more mad. Hey, it's not our fault. It's the rules. If they put up too much of a stink, I might give them their way and then let them know that we don't need their business any longer. The only customers we need are the ones that follow our rules – and since we don't have as many customers as we used to… why, I'm not sure, you won't have as many idiot customers to deal with anyway. Remember, customer service is your most important job! Keep up the good work!"

Does any of this sound familiar? Although I've never seen this policy in print before, I have seen it in action hundreds of times. Does your business have a policy like this? If it does, rip up the imaginary paper that it's written on and give your employees the power to make a difference. It *will* make a difference.

If you're still afraid of empowerment, don't give up on the idea. It's too important. Find ways to empower your employees to make the decisions necessary to serve your customers. If it makes you feel better, develop a system of checks and balances. For example, if you own a restaurant and you empower your wait staff to "do whatever it takes" to please a customer, let them decide if an individual or even a whole table should receive a discount, a complimentary dessert or have their whole bill "comped." You can then have your manager sign off on the transaction with no negative repercussions. Of course, the manager can inquire as to why this needs to be done, but let the wait staff make the decision. Depending on your mindset this may sound simple or complex, enlightening or insane. Regardless, empowerment is critical for world-class service. You decide.

Identify Practical Action Steps

We've established that core beliefs must be a part of your training. But the key is to get them to jump off the page and become real for your employees. Luckily, I happen to know a business that has achieved just that. After such a great experience on my first visit to your imaginary grocery store on my first visit, let's visit again to see how you did it…

Let's go back and review one of your core beliefs:

"The food items in our store will not be presented as mere commodities. The shoppers at our store will be able to experience the tastes, smells, creative uses and presentations of the products we offer."

This statement alone sounds pretty good. And it is. The only thing wrong is that it's just words. You need to turn this core belief into a practical action for your employees so they can turn words into actions that your customers can appreciate.

Having already created a service powerhouse at your grocery store, you've undoubtedly worked through a procedure similar to the one listed below when you created your practical actions...

First, you've submitted this core belief to each of your department managers. They in turn called a meeting with everyone who worked in their department to discuss ways to create practical actions to demonstrate this core belief to their customers. Everyone, from the manager to the newest employee, contributed their ideas. After considering them all, they decided on a few key practical actions that would be their benchmarks for delivering this core belief to their customers.

Most likely, each department in your grocery store interpreted this core belief differently. This is a very good thing for you and your customers. No more one-size-fits-all rules, regulations and procedures. The individuality of each department interpreting what this core belief means to them gives everyone an opportunity to lock into the core beliefs, but at their own level. It makes it real for the employees; they've helped create the practical actions, and now they have ownership of them.

So what type of practical actions did each department create from your core belief?

Core Belief: "The food items in our store will not be presented as mere commodities. The shoppers at our store will be able to experience the tastes, smells, creative uses and presentations of the products we offer."

The Bakery – The bakers felt that although their customers are always interested in new items, they are hesitant to bake something themselves that they've never tried before. So the bakery decided to bring an international flavor to their pastry counter by creating a different international pastry item each week. They published a calendar so their customers would know when the various pastries would be available. Of course, they provided free samples and take-home recipes of everything they baked. The take-home recipe also included the location of all of the necessary ingredients in the store.

The Deli – The deli counter employees knew that the majority of customers buying cold cuts were using them to make sandwiches later that day at home. The deli employees determined that the best way to save their customers' time and to give them the best service possible was not only to sell meat, but to create sandwiches that would be better described as "works of art." So they opened their own sandwich shop right there at the deli counter.

The Children's Play Area – The Children's Play Area entertains children in a secured environment while mom or dad shop. They decided that everyday at noon, they would assist the children in creating a healthy snack using various food items in the store. They would give background information regarding the nutritional values of the various foods used to prepare the recipes. When completed, the children would be able to eat what they created and then be given the recipe and the location of all of the ingredients in the store, in case their mom or dad wanted to buy them to make the recipe at home.

These were just a few of the many outstanding ideas that the different departments came up with to create your *Service with Purpose* company. Each one of your core beliefs generated dozens of practical actions that wowed your customers every time they visited your store. Nice job!

Where do you go from here? Every step in the *Service with Purpose* process continues to move forward and build off what has already been done. This is one of the secrets of its success. There are no dead ends, just a big circle of service that keeps you moving forward. So, once you have established some practical actions that have been agreed upon, it's time to set the standards of what is expected.

Setting Your Standards

You need to know how to play a game in order to win it. Students need to know what they need to study in order to get an "A" on a test. World-class athletes need to know how high they will have to jump, how fast they will need to run or how much weight they will have to lift to win a gold medal. Your children need to know what is expected of them to give them the opportunity to behave properly. Isn't it only fair to give your employees the same opportunities, the same respect? Your employees need to know what is expected of them and how they will be judged. Makes sense, right?

Whether this is obvious or not, if you randomly asked ten front-line employees at ten different businesses if they could name two service goals for their job – or any specific goal for their job for that matter, how many do you think could do it? One, two, probably none.

To keep this from happening to your business, begin by finding ways to measure your practical actions. As much as possible, work with your employees to develop a system of measurement that everyone is happy with and that seems fair and reasonable. You want them to know what needs to be done. Fair and reasonable goals do not necessarily mean easy to attain. Don't be afraid to challenge yourself and your organization by raising the bar to new heights. Once everyone knows what's expected of them and how they will be judged, you've started to create an environment of success for your employees that will reduce turnover, create higher-performing employees and create a plethora of other benefits.

One last thought on training...

When it's all said and done, training will play a huge role in your quest to become a *Service with Purpose* business. Strong training programs will undoubtedly help to reduce turnover and bring your core beliefs to life through practical actions. Despite this, some people suggest the main reason many employees are dissatisfied or leave their jobs is not a lack of training, recognition or financial compensation, but, instead, because of a basic dislike of their boss. Would you like to work for you? Hmmm... Just something to think about.

"If I were a gravedigger there are some people I could work for with a great deal of pleasure."
-Douglas Jerrold

Speaking of you, this may be a good time for a little introspection.

One more last thought...

What kind of manager are you?

Now whether you're a manager by title or not, let's face it – if you're in business, you're a manager. Just about every day you ask someone to do something for you, whether it's a simple task or an elaborate project. The people around you either respond with enthusiasm and energy to your requests or maybe they respond with something less than excitement.

Even if you're a front-line employee, you may ask a co-worker to assist you in restacking the cans of beans on Aisle 12. Does that co-worker help you? Chances are they will if they feel that you are someone who pulls your own weight and that the help is necessary or will be beneficial in some way. They probably won't help you or will only reluctantly do so if they think you're just being bossy person or simply lazy.

The same holds true if you actually are a manager in the service industry. The people who work for you want to know that you're part of the team, not just someone who comes by every once in a while to check on them. It's imperative to become more of a coach and less of a critic. If your employees don't regularly see you in the trenches with them, they are not going to have confidence in you, and you will really nurture the idea of "us versus them." You will be viewed at the typical "suit."

Of course, to be considered a "suit" you don't need to actually be wearing one; you just need to be acting like you are. Make the time to work with the people on the front lines of your business. Talk to them; find out what problems they're having. What are their concerns? If you think you don't have time for this sort of thing because your other responsibilities are too pressing, you're really missing the point.

If you're a manager, you may never hear your employees say that you're lazy or bossy, but that doesn't mean they aren't thinking it or even saying it behind your back. And if they believe this, they are not going to give you their best effort; they may even work against you when they see an opportunity.

"C'mon," you say, "I'm working my tail off on all of this *Service with Purpose* stuff. I take work home. I stay up late – I'm a hard worker!"

You may be. But do you ever leave your office? Do you ever get side by side with your front-liners? Do they ever *see* you work? Do your employees think you're out of touch with what really happens on a daily basis? Depending on your answers to these questions, your employees' perception of you may not be what you would hope it to be. If all you do is pontificate or manage from high atop "Management Mountain," it may be time to step down and spend some time with the people who are in the trenches.

C. Richard Yarbrough, an Atlanta businessman, has this to say about most management:

> "All CEOs espouse good customer service as their number 1 priority in their annual meeting spiels. But that is just so much bull hockey. Most of them are so insulated and isolated from customers by their palace guard that they rarely see, or talk to, a customer."

In my opinion, this isolation isn't limited to customers. You could probably find a great number of managers and management personnel equally isolated from their employees.

From CEOs of large corporations to small business owners, this situation is relatively common. Don't let it be common for you.

Don't ever get too big to be hands on.

The Six Essentials of Service

1 - Vision

2 - Hiring

3 - Training

4 - Communication

5 -

6 -

Chapter 13:

Essential #4

Communication

"I've been visiting the workplaces of America administering a simple test. I call it the 'pronoun test.' I ask frontline workers a few general questions about the company. If the answers I get back describe the company in terms like 'they' and 'them,' then I know it's one kind of company. If the answers are put in terms of 'we' or 'us,' I know it's a different kind of company."

– Robert B. Reich, Former Secretary of Labor

No, it's not the hokey-pokey. Communication is what it's all about!

How many parents have lamented that their teenagers just don't talk to them about anything. They won't let their parents into their lives. Here's a typical teen/parent conversation:

Mom: "How was school today?"

Teenager: "Fine."

Mom: "Did you learn anything interesting?"

Teenager: "Not really."

Mom: "What would you like for dinner?"

Teenager: "Whatever."

Or…

How many millions of times do you think marriage therapists have heard…

"I don't know what happened. We just aren't communicating. I barely know who he/she is anymore."

By now you're probably getting used to all of the personal and family analogies that I've been throwing at you, and I guess they will just keep coming until it finally sinks in that caring is caring – family, friends or customers. In your personal relationships, it's no secret how important communication is; therefore it should come as no surprise that communication with your customers is just as important.

Just about every major family decision involves first discussing the issues with the other members of your family. Even if you will ultimately have the final say on an important family decision, you will most likely still solicit the opinion and guidance of the people around you. If you can't see where this is going, here's a hint...

It should be no different with your customers!

So how do we go about communicating in a business sense? First, remember that listening is always more important than talking. For some people – myself included – this is a difficult pill to swallow. But sometimes, well, you just need to shut up and listen.

Listening and Soliciting Information

Just listen.

How do you listen? Begin simply by paying attention to what people are saying: your employees, your customers, and your vendors. Probably the most important way to start is by listening to your complaints. Or better yet, take it one step further...

Cherish your Complaints

This is a big one. Complaints give you direct, often unsolicited feedback from people using and experiencing your product or service. Although you may believe it to be to the contrary, only about

4% of your customers will complain. The other 96% will just quietly leave or stop doing business with you. Let's make sure that sank in...

Only 4% of your customers with complaints make them. The rest quietly look for something better.

Most complaints will be made to your front-line workers and will never make it any further. It is estimated that only 5-10% of complaints made to employees get passed on to top management. Why would they? Front-line workers don't want their managers to hear about them doing something wrong or have to deal with long, drawn-out explanations to management. And middle managers don't want upper management thinking they're incapable of handling customers in a positive way.

When you consider that most customers keep their complaints to themselves and of those that are made, only a small percentage get passed on to upper management, perhaps only two complaints in 1,000 get passed along to top management. That's unbelievable! But very possible. Are you currently getting tons of complaints, or haven't you heard any in awhile? Either way, it may call for some serious attention.

It's possible that only two complaints in 1,000 get passed along to top management.

Since you have so few opportunities to address complaints as a business, make sure you're set up to receive and evaluate complaints.

What happens when customers do complain? Beyond having a customer politely relay a complaint to you, do you ever have to deal with customers that are cranky, angry or make no sense at all? When upset or irrational, a customer's worth may seem minuscule – or even more of an annoyance than anything else. But when you treat your customers like they have no value, you'll do more than just lose that customer; you'll set a precedent.

Intentionally or unintentionally you'll create an environment that determines which customers are important and which ones are not. It's not long before the entire company senses this mentality and everyone starts qualifying customers. "She was pushy." "He was rude." "They want too much too fast." "They don't understand how things work around here." "He was just too stupid!"

When it becomes okay to lose one customer, it will certainly be accepted that it's okay to lose another.

If you are a manager and a new employee sees you dismiss a customer with a curt response and then silently mouth to your employee, "What a jerk," I can pretty much guarantee the next time your new employee is faced with a similar situation, he is going to treat that customer like a jerk. After all, his boss did.

The ability to receive and handle complaints professionally is important, but an even better skill is to prevent complaints before they even happen. This is why it is so important to continually evaluate and anticipate where problems may arise and address those areas before you have to resolve conflicts with your customers. A little pre-planning on your part can pay huge dividends for everyone who comes in contact with your business.

Pre-empting customers from having a negative experience with your business is a worthwhile endeavor. It used to be said that upset customers would tell anywhere between 10 – 20 people about their negative experience. But with the convenience and power of the Internet, posting a negative experience on a message board or in a chat room doesn't take much effort. All of a sudden that 10 to 20 people has become thousands! Are you prepared to deal with that much negative promotion? Why would you want to?

And what about employee complaints? What are they complaining about? Are they just a bunch of unappreciative, lazy, good-for-nothings? Or is it possible – is there maybe just the slightest chance – that you or your business isn't providing the caring environment that you're shooting for? Are they not receiving necessary training, or are they forced to work with conflicting priorities as we've already discussed?

Listen closely to all of your complaints. They may hold more inside information and wisdom than you ever thought a lazy, good-for-nothing employee or crazy customer could ever provide.

Over time, your observations, questions and evaluations begin to create a picture of how well you're delivering your core beliefs to your customers. In fact if you ask enough of the right questions, and ask them the right way, you may find problems and needs that your customers didn't even know they had.

While it's critical that you ask lots of questions to uncover the problems, remember that the questions are just the first step. It's far more important to seek out the solutions to those problems.

Know your customers

Asking questions, the right kind of questions, is incredibly important. The following scenario could illustrate an example of the wrong type of question.

Edith works at the local diner. As customers approach the cash register to pay their bill, Edith has been instructed by her manager to ask the following question: "How was everything today?"

Ninety-nine percent of the time, the customer replies: "Everything was fine. Thank you."

Customers normally give this response as they hurriedly dig through their pockets looking for the correct change or their car keys as they are preparing to exit the restaurant. It's like when some asks you, "How are you doing today?" You typically reply, "Fine," even if you're having the worst day of your life.

At the end of the day the restaurant manager asks Edith for customer feedback. Edith proudly informs her manager that except for a few customers that were "real idiots," just about everyone said that everything was fine.

The manger confidently smiles and nods in self-satisfaction and never considers changing a thing. "Why fix it if it ain't broke?" he thinks to himself.

Amazingly, the same week that I was working on this chapter and writing the fictitious story above, I had a real-life experience that really summed up these situations.

My family had gone out for dinner to a home-style national chain restaurant. Our meals were delicious, but the service was poor. We waited and waited and waited. First we waited for our waitress to take our order and then for our food to be served. While we weren't motivated to complain, we all talked about it amongst ourselves.

When we finally finished our dining experience, I took the bill to the cashier. Go ahead.... Guess what she said... She asked me, "How was everything today?"

Just as in my fictitious story above, I robotically replied, "Fine."

Then I remembered this chapter, and to protect the restaurant from their own stupid question, I regrouped and added, "You know the food was good, but we really had to wait way too long to be served. It was kind of ridiculous actually." I felt pretty good after giving a thoughtful answer to her question. After all, how could they improve if all I said was "Fine"? I was feeling pretty good until I heard her response. "I'm sorry to hear that, sir. Your total today is $44.59."

Stunned and disheartened, I handed over the money and quietly shuffled out the door.

Don't train your employees to ask your customers stupid questions if they aren't interested in the answers.

Please, don't let this happen to you. You must take the time to train your front-liners to honestly find out what your customers want and what they like or dislike about your service. And just as importantly, you must encourage them to sincerely care about your customers' responses to the questions they ask.

Sometimes it can be especially uncomfortable to find out what customers don't like about your business. After all, who likes looking for problems? For example, everyone knows that it's wise to visit your doctor for physicals on a regular basis. They make sure everything is working properly and if there is a problem, it can be discovered early so it can be treated. But why don't more people go for their regular check-ups? Why do some people refuse to go to the doctor altogether? The answer is that very few people like to go digging around for problems. "Everything seems to be working okay – so lets just go with that."

It's a mistake made by seemingly healthy individuals and businesses alike. They feel it would be like asking their doctor, "Can't you run just one more test? I feel fine, but you must be able to find a problem somewhere. C'mon, keep looking." Most people feel that if it's not broken, why fix it? But if there is a problem that you're unaware of and it goes untreated, it can only get worse. Be willing to stand up and find the problems in your business now, before they become untreatable. Ask questions, even if the answers may be difficult for you to hear.

One of the ways you can unwillingly hide from the truth is by asking your customer if everything was "Okay."

What Kinds of Questions Should I Ask?

How do you find out what's important to your customers? How do you know if they most want low price, high quality, speed, or simplicity of use? Maybe your customers want something more intangible like trust, integrity or relationships?

Answers to questions like these need to be uncovered by digging deeply. When you take the time to learn about your customers and implement what you uncovered, you become more than just a supplier of goods or services; you become an extension of your customers' life. You become someone they know they can depend on to find the answers, products or services they need. Simply stated, if you learn what your customers want and consistently give it to them, they'll keep coming back.

When you ask your customers enough of the right questions, you'll eventually be able to *anticipate* their needs. When you can do this effectively, your customers will be "wowed."

Following are some examples of different types of evaluation that can be used to determine your customers' needs and how well your business is meeting and exceeding them:

Observation

Simply watch how things are being done. Does it appear that you are operating at a level that is close to your original vision? Basically, how do things look to you? Take notes on what you see and refer back to them often. Sometimes the changes that need to be made can be subtle and can only be uncovered by comparing your notes over a period of time.

Internal surveying

Start by simply asking your employees how they think things are going. Ask managers how their team members are doing. Ask team members how their managers are doing. Ask everyone how *you* are doing (gulp).

Develop evaluation forms and suggestion cards and make them available to your employees. Make sure that confidentiality is a part of the process when it's appropriate.

"The key to success is to get out into the store and listen to what the associates have to say. It's terribly important for everyone to get involved. Our best ideas come from clerks and stockboys."
– Sam Walton, Wal-Mart founder

Customer Surveying

Talk to your customers BEFORE, DURING and AFTER dealing with you. Watch them. Listen to them. Their perceptions are your reality.

BEFORE: What are their needs and expectations? Where have they done business before? Why did they choose you this time?

DURING: Do you have their best interests in mind when you're making the sale? Are you giving the customer your full attention? Does the customer feel important and comfortable when interacting with you, or are they just treated like the next person in line?

AFTER: Have you followed up with your customers? Did you ask if their experience was a positive or a negative one? Why was it good or bad?

Focus Groups

Regularly gather a group of your customers (both past and present, if possible) and have them share their likes and dislikes of your product or service.

Ask lots of open-ended, thought-provoking questions. For example,

"If there was one new product/service we could provide for you, what would you want it to be?"

"Do you ever do business with our competitors? Why?"

"What's your favorite thing about our product/service?" "What's your least favorite?"

The questions are nearly endless. The information (put to good use) is invaluable.

Mystery Shoppers

All companies already have mystery shoppers in place; they're just not aware of it. Yes, you even have them where you work. I know you didn't hire any, but you still have them. They're called your customers. They come in and evaluate you and judge your products and services. Unfortunately, often the only feedback you'll receive from them is when they silently stop spending their money with you because you've stopped meeting their needs.

There are companies, however, that provide professional mystery shoppers. They can be extremely helpful in giving you an objective view of your company's service and overall operations.

To this point, we've been discussing how important it is for you to gather information, to seek out others' opinions and to listen when they give them. As we've discussed, listening is a vital part of successful communication. But true communication is not a one-way street. It takes place between you, your employees and your customers, and it flows in all directions. You continually gather new information in a never-ending quest to improve. But just as important as collecting information is providing feedback to your customers and employees.

Providing Feedback

Soliciting information and providing feedback are both extremely important elements that make up the discipline of communication. But when using one without the other, they become nearly worthless. Combining these two elements is required in successful communication. Used in conjunction, they create a very powerful tool. Used individually, they will produce few results and may even become counter-productive.

People do not appreciate taking their time to give you their opinions if they never see any benefit in doing so. Nor do they like participating in an evaluation and never knowing the results of that evaluation. On a more obvious level, why would you take the time to collect information as a business if you're not going to use it? Don't waste your customers' and employees' time and don't waste your time and money collecting information that you don't use. Keep in mind: your good intentions don't count. If you're going to inquire and evaluate, then you must give feedback, and vice-versa.

On evaluating performance, employees don't like being evaluated and not knowing if they were evaluated positively or negatively. So don't keep secrets from your employees. Let everyone know that they will be evaluated and what criteria are being used. If possible, show your employees the evaluation form. Better yet, have them help to create it. Give your employees every opportunity to succeed.

If, in a nutshell, you use evaluations to determine who gets raises and who gets fired, and you don't share the results of your evaluations with your employees, you may not be helping your cause. When one of your top performers receives a raise because your "secret" evaluations said he should, and then he is later asked why he received that raise, there's a very good chance that he's not going to know.

"Because I work hard?" the employee might say in a somewhat quizzical voice. That is probably at least partially true, but too vague to be a motivational factor for the employee. It's very difficult to train people to work hard if they don't know exactly what "work hard" means. In your business, does working hard involve working quickly and getting a lot done, or working slowly and precisely? If the position requires more physical labor, maybe you judge how hard an employee is working based on if they look sweaty or tired, or maybe it's the ability to lift heavy things? In an office, it can mean answering many phone calls or completing mountains of paperwork. What does working hard mean to you? Do your employees know what *your* definition of a "hard worker" is?

Wouldn't it be productive for the employee to know that he excels in delivering your core beliefs to you customers and can rattle off two or three key practical actions that he continually focuses on? This employee knows why he deserved his raise. And if he wants another one, he knows what actions are required of him. Giving raises or any rewards without some kind of justification is not going to improve the overall performance, morale or caring culture of your business.

If you want to super charge your employees, take your core beliefs to the next level. Beyond simply training your employees to be able to recite your core beliefs, make it clear to them how what they do makes a difference. Does your employee think she is simply picking up trash in the dining area, or is she assuring your customers that your dining room will always be as clean as their dining room in their own home? How your employees perceive what they do is incredibly important.

> *"If what you're working for really matters, you'll give it all you've got."*
> -Nido Qubein

When your employees know why your business exists and how they are a part of it all – look out! If you've achieved this level of understanding between you and your employees, you're operating in the top tenth of 1% of all businesses in the world. (I just made that statistic up, but it's probably pretty close.)

Providing positive feedback is great, but feedback is also important for employees who are not performing well. Good or bad, you want your employees to know specifically where they need to improve and you want them to have every opportunity to succeed. If unfortunately an employee needs to be terminated, at least both of you will know how the situation came to this end. But let's not dwell on the negative.

Three Types of Feedback

There are basically three types of feedback you can provide to your employees. The first is providing positive feedback, which would include giving raises or providing recognition. Whether it is an award, certificate or an "Atta boy!" – it's letting someone know that their efforts are being recognized and appreciated.

Second, you can provide negative feedback. Reprimanding, yelling or making an employee feel poorly about something they've done or not done. In a milder form, it would also include respectfully correcting an employee who is performing below expectations.

The third type of feedback available to you – and probably the most used – is providing no feedback at all. Yes, you read that right. *No* feedback is a form of feedback.

If you randomly visited businesses or observed managers at work, you would most likely discover that most feedback is dispensed in the following order. First, most managers will either provide too little feedback or no feedback at all. The second most common type of feedback used is negative. And the least used, most important and most beneficial type of feedback is positive feedback.

It unfortunately comes in a distant third to the other two.

Three types of feedback:
Positive, Negative & None

Let's see how each approach would play out at a local fast food restaurant...

Steve is the newest employee at the House of Burgers. He has been assigned to work on dining room cleanup.

Steve thinks his job is ridiculously easy so he only pays the slightest attention to what he is doing. He spends most of his time daydreaming as he wonders around the dining room, squirting the dirty tables with his spray bottle and twirling his dirty rag once or twice on the tabletops. Clean or not, he moves on to the next dirty table.

His manager notices how sloppily he is wiping off the tables and gently corrects Steve. In typical coaching fashion, the manager explains that many of the customers who come to the House of Burgers do so because of the restaurant's reputation for cleanliness. The manager explains further that demonstrating effort and ability in these simple assignments will quickly lead to more responsibility and possibly a raise. Lastly, the manager lets Steve know that he expects improvement in the future. Steve knew he wasn't doing his best so he wasn't surprised to receive the negative feedback.

Steve started doing a much better job as soon as he understood the restaurant's core beliefs and specific practical actions that he needed to utilize. Steve's ongoing training taught him that although parts of his job seemed trivial and simplistic, his responsibilities were imperative to the overall success of the restaurant. His manager soon took notice and complimented Steve on his attitude and general improvement along with specific actions that Steve was doing particularly well.

Over time, Steve's manager did so well in creating a *Service with Purpose* restaurant that he was promoted to regional manager. Before he left, he advised the new store manager that Steve deserved more responsibility and a raise. But Steve's new manager was brought from outside of the organization and wasn't familiar with *Service with Purpose* philosophies and managed without much concern for the people around him. He rarely gave any feedback and when he did it was negative. When the manager started his new position, he had enough problems of his own and didn't have time to train Steve or worry about giving raises. But Steve patiently worked on.

The new manager noticed that Steve was doing a good job, but figured that it was Steve's responsibility to do a good job. "Why should you make a big deal about something they're supposed to do?" the manager was often heard to say. Steve began to notice that the only time he ever heard anything from his new manager was when something was wrong. Months went by and Steve was still wiping tables as his manager often shouted across the dining room, "Hey, you missed one!"

Over time, what do you think happened to Steve's performance? How much longer do you think Steve's career lasted at the House of Burgers? Most likely, how was the morale of the other employees at the restaurant?

This scenario is played over and over again in businesses of all shapes and sizes every day of every year. Don't allow yourself to fall victim to this service killer.

Recognize good work and you strengthen a person's desire to improve. Don't recognize good work and fuel an employee's most common frustration – a lack of recognition.

How does this relate to a caring business philosophy? What if your son or daughter continually brings home outstanding report cards and no one makes a big deal about it, because after all, children are supposed to get good grades. Unfortunately, the only time your child hears anything from you is when they receive a grade that's not so good.

"You need to work on that. Spend more time studying." Or if you're really tough they might get grounded. After a while, what's your child's attitude going to be like? See? Caring is caring.

So for your *Service with Purpose* business, you're going to reverse this scenario. You will provide far more positive feedback than anything else. And by the way, if your child has improved her English grade from a "D" to a "C," make sure you let her know that you're proud of her. Keep that positive feedback flowing! Accentuate the positive at every opportunity.

This is not a minor point to be glossed over. So, one more time… Accentuate the positive at every opportunity.

Nice Job, But…

If you're not prone to giving positive feedback, but you're trying to improve, watch out for the biggest trap of all in positive feedback: The proverbial "Nice job, but…" The "but" negates everything positive you might have said and makes the person you were complimenting feel like you just softened them up with kind words before you criticized their performance. Which, from your employee's perspective, was the only reason you complimented him in the first place. When you're being positive, keep it positive. Don't turn a positive feeling into an opportunity to correct someone.

The Six Essentials of Service

1 - Vision

2 - Hiring

3 - Training

4 - Communication

5 - Recognition

6 -

Chapter 14:

Essential #5

Recognition

Surprise!

        Great Job!

                Thank you!

                        Great Idea!

The discipline of recognition is an outward expression of appreciation for the people who make your business work. It's about how you reward and celebrate your employees for their efforts. It's about how you share your business' achievements, both big and small.

Listed at the beginning of this chapter are just a few of the ways to verbally recognize the people you work with and to let them know that they're appreciated. But recognition is not limited to your employees; it is just as important for your customers and vendors. From the "free suckers on the counter" for your youngest customers to special events for your best customers, it doesn't always matter what you do as long as you do something that shows sincere appreciation.

With employees, if you insist, you can still be one of those dinosaurs who suggest, "People should just be happy that they have a job. And besides, they get paid to be here! They shouldn't need any more encouragement than that." If you think that way, well then, um – stop it.

If you are inclined to recognize your employees, and I hope you are, here are two different approaches.

Awards

An award can be an item like a trophy, plaque or certificate given to an individual or a team to commemorate a specific achievement or reaching a goal. An award can also be a cash prize or be an item of monetary value.

Celebration

This form of recognition is available to everyone because it's free and it's effective. Simple recognition can be verbal or written praise in acknowledgment of an individual's or team's achievement. When delivered consistently and sincerely, simple recognition can be the most appreciated and powerful of all recognition types.

"I can live two months on a good compliment."
— Mark Twain

You don't need a huge budget to start recognizing your employees. Small signs of appreciation consistently delivered can be even more effective than an elaborate one-time event.

"People respond to something that costs little or nothing and that something is called recognition."
— Edward Lawler

In his book *Life Positive*, author Tim Olney states that, "Twelve roses are better than a dozen." His contention is that giving a single rose on twelve different occasions will provide twelve individual opportunities to show your appreciation, instead of just one. It makes sense. If you can't afford the big stuff, do what you can. Good life philosophies and good business philosophies mirror each other time after time.

So What Do They Want?

If you're a business owner or manager and you've decided to provide awards to your employees that have a monetary value, you probably can't afford to give your employees things that won't be appreciated or valued. If you're going to give anything for recognition, make sure you give something that has perceived value. The key term here is "perceived value." As we've already discussed, recognition does not have to be expensive, just valued. In some companies a lapel pin or certificate is a highly coveted award when it is difficult to attain.

If you are going to invest money in your employees' awards, don't spend your money foolishly. The key to successfully recognizing your employees with awards that have monetary value is to find out the types of things that interest and are important to them.

To illustrate this point, did you ever receive a birthday gift from a family member with whom you rarely have any contact? These are the relatives you only see on obscure holidays and family events. Despite this lack of contact, every year they remember to send you something on your birthday. Of course, no matter how bad the gift is, a few days later you make the mandatory "thank you call," expressing your gratitude and explaining how you really needed a wall clock that barks like a dog every hour.

We all receive bad gifts from time to time and they usually wind up tossed into the closet – or worse. But the thing to remember is that this gift was given to you for the right reasons – probably because someone cared about you. While you're appreciative that someone took the time to give you something, the gift itself didn't have much perceived value because the gift-giver didn't know enough about you to give you what you wanted.

Another disadvantage of rewarding your employees without their input or understanding them is that they may not think of you, their boss, as "family." They won't have the same appreciation for your efforts as they would a family member.

"I busted my butt for 6 months on this project and they give me a frozen turkey?! You gotta be kidding me!"

I'm not saying turkeys are bad, just make sure they are appropriate to the task being rewarded and that they are appreciated by the recipient. If you're going to make the investment in rewarding people, you want it to be effective. Also, you certainly don't want to create negative attitudes in your employees by giving them rewards that make them feel under appreciated. There's nothing worse than trying to do something nice for people and having it turn out badly.

While recognition focuses on giving rewards rather than giving gifts, the thought process is the same. The only difference is that rewards must be earned (gifts are still nice though). An inappropriate reward will be received just as poorly as an inappropriate gift.

Providing awards with monetary value to your employees without knowing their likes and interests – despite your best intentions – may not provide the results you were hoping for.

So how do you know what your employees would appreciate? Ask them. Discuss your rewards program with your employees. Solicit their ideas and get their feedback. You could also create a voluntary Personal Interest Form. Ask about hobbies, interests, and favorite vacation destinations. When it comes time to reward an employee, you can use this form to determine what type of award may be most appropriate.

It's Okay to Have Fun

The ways in which you recognize your employees is only limited by your imagination and your creativity. Recognizing your employees doesn't always have to be structured and perfectly organized. It's okay to invent new and fun ways to brighten someone's day. Following are a couple of ideas for you.

Fun Stops

These are actions or activities that are completely unexpected. You can do something as simple as bringing in doughnuts or bagels for breakfast or an unplanned pizza party at lunch. It does not have to be associated with performance. It can be for no reason at all other than it makes people feel good about their company and the people they work for and with. Keep things loose; let people know that it's okay to have fun and that they're appreciated. The number of Fun Stops you can come up with is unlimited – let your imagination run wild.

Unexpected Recognition

For most of us, our natural inclination is to catch people doing things wrong. Managers have become very adept at pointing out employees' shortcomings and correcting them right there on the spot. Unexpected recognition is the complete opposite of that philosophy. Instead of watching for people doing things wrong, it becomes your mission to find employees doing something right. For example, as a manager you witness an employee going out of her way to help a customer. You immediately go over to the employee and give her a $10, $20 or $50 bill, or place a star on her nametag. Or it can be as simple as letting the employee know that you just witnessed her doing something great and you appreciate her efforts.

The key to this type of recognition is consistency and the *immediacy* of the reward. For the maximum effect, the reward should be given to the employee as soon as possible following his outstanding performance.

As with everything else, using one of these recognition types once or twice a year isn't going to produce the results you're looking for. Employees need to know that this type of appreciation is a part of your business culture, not just a sporadic blip on the radar. It's all about consistency, consistency, consistency.

> *"People don't do good things just once a year."*
> -Ray Frankowski, Westinghouse

Over time, these displays of recognition will demonstrate to your employees that you sincerely care about them. You're not just doing something nice for them because you need a favor or you need everyone to work overtime. You use these recognition styles regularly to show your appreciation. If your employees know you care, they are much more likely to be motivated to work for you, and with you.

"Employees are strong believers in the old saying, 'It's the thought that counts,' and for awards to count as recognition, employees need to see acknowledgment of their specific accomplishments and sincere appreciation of their personal value to the organization."

– Cindy Ventrice, author of *Make Their Day!*

Make your efforts pay off

In his book, *Managing To Have Fun*, author Matt Weinstein gives an excellent example of a fun and effective reward program used by a dentist to motivate his staff.

> After a profitable month, a dentist decided that it would be appropriate to give each of his employees a $200 bonus for their recent efforts. If this was a typical business, the bonus would simply be added to everyone's paycheck and the bonus would quickly get gobbled up by the employees' bills, groceries and other daily expenses. Although the $200 would have been appreciated, it would soon be forgotten, as money itself is pretty emotionless.
>
> To prevent this from happening, the dentist made his $200 bonuses come alive. One day, he took his staff

to the mall and handed each one of them an envelope containing $200. The dentist then stated that this was his money and there were some rules attached to it. First, the employees only had one hour to spend their $200. After one hour they were to meet at a specified location. Second, they could only spend the money on themselves and had to buy at least 5 different items. The last stipulation was that whatever money hadn't been spent in that hour had to be returned to the dentist.

The results were just as the dentist had hoped. The employees enjoyed their shopping spree while taking part in a team-building event in a very positive environment. Undoubtedly, it was an event that the employees will remember for years to come.

Can you see how much more productive that bonus money has become? If you're going to spend money or take the time to reward and recognize your employees, do it right. Don't think you have to do it exactly like the dentist did; there are hundreds of ideas like this one. Take the time to find one that's right for your company and your budget.

Employee Motivation

Everyone is motivated to do something. Granted, some people are only motivated to sit on the couch, but nevertheless they are motivated to sit there. People are driven to activity (or inactivity) because they are either doing something that brings them pleasure or moves them away from pain or an unpleasant situation.

Be a little introspective and examine your daily decisions and you reveal your own motivations. It's really quite fascinating. Do you dread returning phone calls so you let them sit on your desk for days? Do you procrastinate on putting your sales report together? Have you delayed starting that diet you keep talking about? Why do you do it? It's all about moving toward something pleasurable or away from something unpleasant.

Let's say you want to lose some weight so you sign up at the gym. But when the day comes for you to go and work out, something comes up unexpectedly so you can't go. You're surprised to find that you seem to have things "coming up" just about every time you try to go work out. Why does this happen? Unless you have legitimate reasons (be honest), the contemplation of the pain and "exhaustedness" that come from starting a workout routine is greater than the pleasure of staying at home and watching television or imagining your body looking lean and healthy.

The same thinking applies to your employees. The reason you can't "convince" your employees to act or respond in desired ways is because people will only do things that they perceive will benefit them in some way.

From that perspective, there are two types of motivation at work in all of us. The one that is easiest to initiate in business and is most commonly used by managers is *extrinsic* motivation. Extrinsic motivation utilizes external influences to encourage and reward employees. Things like bonuses or other monetary compensation are most common, but any tangible reward or incentive would fit this bill. An employee does a job well or completes a particular task and he is rewarded for his efforts. This is a "dangling-the-carrot" type of motivation.

The other type of motivation is *intrinsic*. Intrinsic motivation comes from our own internal factors. Traits like pride, feeling "in on things," and having a strong desire to do well are motivational factors that come from inside us. Managers cannot demand employees to have these types of feelings and attitudes toward their work, but they can create an environment that is conducive to creating these types of feelings.

Although intrinsic motivation cannot be coaxed out of your employees, many employers still feel they can command their employees to "smile and be friendly." But let's face it, if your employees aren't happy, telling them to smile isn't going to do the trick. But *Service with Purpose* is not something about which people need to be convinced. It's about doing things every day that show you care about your employees and your customers.

Build Extrinsic and Intrinsic Motivation into Your Programs

The best organizations use both extrinsic and intrinsic motivation and are aware of the necessity to have them both working in conjunction with each other. According to Bob Nelson, author of *1001 Ways To Reward Employees*, you can build intrinsic motivation into your existing reward program by following three guidelines.

1) **Set goals that will have mutual benefit for the company and the employee.**

Surprisingly, that "benefit" isn't always money. In fact, presenting an employee with an opportunity for career advancement, learning a new skill or more responsibility may be more motivating than a token raise. This type of customized goal setting works best when mutually agreed upon with each individual employee, encouraging his ideas and initiative as much as possible.

2) Partner in the achievement of goals.

Managers' roles continue to change from being the "boss" to the "coach." Let your employees know that you are on their side in regards to achieving goals by offering consistent praise, encouragement and assistance whenever possible. One of the additional benefits to coaching is that most employees indicate they are more motivated by personal recognition from their managers or in written form than by more formal incentives.

3) Allow for individual choice in rewards.

As we've already discussed, this means asking employees what they would consider motivating if they achieved certain goals at work. Maybe give them some parameters, like choosing items that range in cost from $25 to $200. When the time comes to recognize your staff, you won't have to wonder if they're going to like the frozen turkey you were planning on giving them. Instead of handing out commonplace prizes, your employees may choose tickets to concerts or sporting events, limousine rentals or half days off. People work harder for things they want. Wouldn't you?

Instead of understanding motivation, more often than not, managers will try to coax, bribe or prod their employees into doing something that they want done. Obviously, this widely used "coaxing" method doesn't work very well. How do I know that? Well…

most people use this technique and crummy service is epidemic. Coincidence? I think not.

"If your employee is not performing as expected – is it because you hired them that way or made them that way after you hired them?"

-W. Edwards Deming

"The key to great customer service is a satisfied employee."

-Roger Dow, Marriott Hotels & Resorts

You're Certifiable!

If you've made it this far and you've found that you really want to make this work then, yes, YOU'RE CERTIFIABLE! No don't worry, no rubber rooms for you. You're certifiable in a good way. You're S.M.I.L.E. Certified. S.M.I.L.E. is an acronym for *Service Mastery through Individual Levels of Excellence.*

In previous chapters, I've said that you can't become a *Service with Purpose* business without the support of your whole team and this is true.

Whether or not you're a sports fan, you've probably had an opportunity to watch a football game or two. Football is a great example of how a team works together, or not. For instance, if a team is comprised of one superstar player and a bunch of scrubs, you've probably got a losing team on your hands. BUT, if you have a *team* of individuals, all giving 100 percent – even if none of them are superstars – well then, we might be talking Super Bowl, baby!

All successful teams are built on the successful contributions of individuals toward a common goal. SMILE certification is all about promoting individual accomplishments toward a team goal.

For example, if you operate a fast-food restaurant, you know how profitable soft drink sales can be. To increase revenues, you devise a plan to sell more. You normally sell about 500 drinks per day, but you'd like to sell about 650. So you hang a big banner in your kitchen that reads, "Whoever sells the most drinks this week receives 2 free movie tickets!" Since you know that your employees *love* going to the movies, you think you've got a winning idea.

It sounds good; your intentions are good. But if your business is like most, you'll have two or three employees who will really get excited and go all out. The others will just assume that they'll never keep up with those who are really trying, so what do they do? They don't try at all. Why would they? They assume they cannot win so they continue to sell the same amount of drinks without any improvement. This "whoever-does-the-most" type of goal creates "superstars," but as our football analogy explained, your chances of winning are much greater with a total team effort.

So how do you build a team and still encourage individual levels of excellence? Start by reviewing what you know about goal setting. In this scenario, you may want to set two different goals – an individual goal and a team goal.

To keep things simple, let's assume that every day you have about ten people working the register at your restaurant. Based on selling about 500 drinks per day, you know that each cashier sells about 50 drinks. To achieve your goal of 650 drinks per day, each cashier would need to sell about 15 more drinks. So you develop an individual goal that could read something like this…

"If you sell an average of 65 drinks per shift over the next ten days, you will earn… (Fill in the blank – an extra hour of paid break, a movie ticket, whatever is valuable to your employees.)

The situation you have now is that while this is an individual goal, everyone can attain it. Everyone can sell 65 drinks per day. In this case, the extrinsic goal is the reward, the prize you are offering. But the fact that an employee can achieve a goal and feel good about himself is intrinsic motivation.

Isn't this great? Everybody wins!

Now for your team goal you could hang a poster that reads...

"Taco Hut Drink Goal for the Week: 4,550 Bever-ages Served. If we hit the goal, everyone is invited to an after-hours pizza party next Friday. Good luck, everybody! I know you can do it!"

Now you're cookin' with gas! Your drink sales will start to improve. Oh, in case you were wondering...

65 drinks x 7 days = 4,550 drinks

Take time to develop your own S.M.I.L.E. certification pro-cess. Tie it to whatever behaviors, attitudes or actions you want, as long as it's tied to an overall team goal or your core beliefs.

One of the S.M.I.L.E. certifications that I have used in the past was a "Going the Extra Smile" award, issued to employees who were caught going above and beyond the call of duty in making a customer's experience extra special. Employees could nominate managers and managers could nominate employees. It wasn't com-plicated, expensive or time consuming. But it was a fun, feel-good award that kept customer care on the minds of employees as they worked their shifts.

When used properly, recognition is a powerful tool that can pay great dividends. Take every opportunity possible to recognize the individuals and teams in your business who help achieve your goals and bring your core beliefs to life.

The Six Essentials of Service

1 - Vision

2 - Hiring

3 - Training

4 - Communication

5 - Recognition

6 - Revision

Chapter 15:

Essential #6

Revision

"Even if at first you succeed, you still have to work hard to stay there."

-Richard C. Miller

Many people believe that "success breeds success." Quite often this is true – at least in the short term. But if you're not careful, success can also breed complacency.

As I stated at the beginning, most people in business think they've got customer service figured out. They know how it all works and they believe without question that their business provides unprecedented service. Ah, for so many, ignorance is bliss! It is most often the companies that *think* they have nothing more to learn regarding customer service that are the furthest away from actually providing *Service with Purpose* for their customers.

You, on the other hand, have taken the time to read these pages, absorb their messages, and have started applying the power of this new service paradigm to your daily business practices. *Service with Purpose* will take you to a new level of success. But once you're on your way, don't get complacent. Understand going in that you're never going to have it "all figured out." Markets and people will always change. Nothing ever stays the same – except for the fact that caring never goes out of style.

Just as you would build a new home on a strong foundation, the same is true of building your business philosophies on a foundation of caring. Over time, you may redecorate your home, knock out a wall, do some painting, replace carpeting, and even change the landscaping outside. But if your foundation is strong, that will remain unchanged.

 You'll never have it all figured out, because nothing ever stays the same.

"When you are green, you grow – when you're ripe, you rot."

-Ray Kroc

In terms of *Service with Purpose*, revision is about maintaining and updating your service vision, just as you would update your home. Revision occurs on two levels. First, because you have your finger on the pulse of your service culture, you should have a good sense of how things are going. If need be, you would be able to make modifications on the fly.

Make no mistake about it, changes will be required.

One of the reasons for this is that every business is going to find itself at various levels of proficiency for each discipline. For example, some companies may do an outstanding job hiring people who fit the service needs of their organization, while their training may be lacking in some areas. Other organizations may do well with most of the essentials but have no strong vision to tie it all together. As your *Service with Purpose* identity grows and matures, you'll continually uncover areas that may need to be "tweaked," or that may even require major overhauls.

About every six months, take time to stop and reflect, review and revise. This way, nothing ever goes unchecked for long periods of time. And it will help your business prevent the development of large service failures. Stop to examine how far you have come since the inception of your original vision. Take note of all the successes and disappointments that have developed around it.

When you're working on the essential of revision, you'll want to take your time and do more than just think about how things are going as you drive to work. I recommend that you do a written evaluation of your progress. Begin with your vision and your core beliefs. If they're not in front of you (where they need to be in order for you to be successful), pull them out and read them again. Internalize them. Keep them on the top of your mind as you analyze the other essentials.

For your written review, list essentials two through five (hiring, training, communication, recognition) at the top of four sheets of paper. For example, one sheet of paper would have "Hiring" listed as the header. On this page, list the ways in which you have specifically changed your hiring practices since implementing *Service with Purpose*. Be specific. Have you changed the type of questions asked, the format of your job application, or the location or types of questions used in your interview? Most importantly, how have things changed to better reflect and deliver your core beliefs to your customers? Have they changed at all?

If your actions are not aligned with your core beliefs you won't experience the results you're seeking – period.

Follow this same exercise with the essentials of Training, Communication and Recognition.

If you find that despite your best efforts something just isn't working, don't be stubborn. If you've taken the time to develop your core beliefs, the changes will most likely be made only in the way you deliver service to your customers, your employees and your vendors – not to your core beliefs. If an idea that you thought was absolutely ingenious (even if you do say so yourself) just isn't working, that's okay. Change is a part of life and a part of the *Service with Purpose* company. The point is that you should never just accept something that isn't right. Never settle. If your core beliefs are sound, you're probably headed in the right direction, although your route may need to be slightly adjusted.

In business, there is no standing still. You are either moving ahead or falling behind.

The important thing is that you continue to learn and grow.

A competitive business market will not allow you to rest on your laurels. The Six Essentials of Service are designed to keep your company in a constant state of improvement. You will be continually focused on ways to improve your company for your customers and the people who make it happen. Former Director of Customer Service at Air Miles Ltd., Larry Hochman believes "Standing still is a terminal illness." Keep moving, keep improving. Be a positive force for all who come in contact with you or your business.

You began this process in the hopes of improving the service your company provides and in doing so, you've hopefully discovered that great service cannot be demanded of your employees. It can be encouraged and demonstrated. By surrounding yourself with positive people, establishing common goals that everyone can work toward, providing ongoing training with lots of feedback, and maintaining a pleasant workplace, you create the fertile soil where the flowers of service will bloom year after year. (Pretty poetic, don't you think?)

If you have initiated the Six Essentials of Service and have worked consistently and with purpose, you will begin to see all of these exciting things starting to happen in your business.

While this process is never completed, each time you work through these essentials, you give yourself the opportunity to improve. Know that even a minor improvement is a success. Continually revise the way you deliver service to the people you care about: your customers. Your unrelenting desire to improve will transform your company in the eyes of all who come in contact with it.

Consider this...

If each time you go through the Six Essentials and make slight revisions, your company becomes only 1 percent better, what could that mean to your company? One measly percent, compounded over and over again, begins to add up over time. The results will be unbelievable!

And better yet, it's doable!

Hiring

_____

_____

_____

_____

Training

_____

_____

_____

_____

Communication

_____

_____

_____

_____

Recognition

_____

_____

_____

_____

Chapter 16:

Doing What You Can to Make a Difference

So now you're really putting it all together. But exactly what you're "putting together" may vary dramatically depending on what role you play within your company. What a CEO would do may be different than what a shift manager would do. But both roles are vitally important to the overall success of *Service with Purpose*. Obviously, the higher the *Service with Purpose* mentality goes up the corporate ladder (even if it's a very short ladder), the better off everyone will be. That's not to say if you're a manager practicing *Service with Purpose* with no support from upper management that you can't make a difference – because you can and you will. You will control what you can control.

For example, as a manager, you may not be able to control the policies of your company. You may have little or no control over the procedures you must follow, but you may have the ability to make decisions about the people who work for you. So you could hire people who would support your vision.

Your vision for your department would consist of the things that you can control. Maybe this would include providing additional training and feedback for your employees or doing a small-scale survey of your customers. If your budget is limited, you could come up with inexpensive ways to celebrate and recognize your employees.

Is it possible that, as a manager, bad policies and decisions at a corporate level could work against you? Absolutely. Thousands of frustrated, customer-centered managers have service obstacles put in front of them at every turn. Many of these managers feel their main job is to do everything they can to work around the service obstacles without getting fired. It may be unnecessary policies, pointless bureaucracy, or a million other things. The point is that now at least you are maximizing what you can do with the cards you've been dealt. And who knows? Maybe your department will become the blueprint that your entire organization will eventually follow.

Many Layers of Service Opportunities

Of course the ideal situation is when a CEO or business owner embraces these philosophies including the Six Essentials of Service and shares them with everyone in the company. When any initiative is supported from the top, it stands a much better chance to succeed than when a few enthusiastic managers must struggle to make a difference without the support and encouragement of upper management. But when this caring philosophy and the accompanying disciplines are encouraged and taught throughout the company, *Service with Purpose* begins to operate at many levels within an organization.

For example, in terms of achieving a company's vision, the responsibilities and goals of a regional manager will differ from a store manager or a front-line worker. Therefore, at each level of the business, from management to operations, the Six Essentials of Service would be at work, but at each level, the methods used in training, communication and even recognition may be handled differently while still striving to fulfill the company's vision in their own way. This becomes another way the efforts of everyone are more personalized, transforming the big picture of the company's vision into images and actions that employees know they can impact. A situation like this becomes very rewarding for employees and incredibly rewarding for the company that makes it happen.

Chapter 17:

So Who Cares?

Well, here we are. The end of the book. So who cares?

Hopefully you do, and you understand the power behind a *Service with Purpose* business strategy and how to implement it for your company or department.

Items covered in this book are not new or revolutionary. They have all been discussed elsewhere in one form or another. So don't fall into the trap of, "Oh, I've heard all of this before," because contrary to popular belief, knowledge is not power. It is in the implementation of knowledge that you'll find the power. So if you have heard it all before – great! Start putting it to use. Put *all* of it to use and create some service magic.

Remember, the key is the Six Essentials, the right mix of all of the ingredients to create a culture of service with your people, procedures and policies – all built on a foundation of caring.

Each of the Six Essentials must be at work in your business to create *Service with Purpose.*

If you still don't care, I have two words for you – Page One!

In a nutshell, one last time here it is…

- Build your business on a foundation of caring.
- Concentrate on each of the Six Essentials of Service every day.
- Remember the Three P's of Service. (Planning, Procedures & People)
- Continue to learn more about hiring, training (including creating practical actions and setting goals), communication (collecting customer feedback, etc.) and recognition (celebrating achievement and having fun at work), and evaluate the information you gather through your core beliefs.

The great news is that while this may seem like a lot of work, the return on investment will be tremendous. Ask yourself, "What if my biggest competitor actually read this book and created a *Service with Purpose* company?" Would you really want to compete against them? I don't think so. Beat them to the punch and unleash "the hounds of caring" on them before they do it to you. That's how you kill your competition with kindness!

Hopefully, you'll find that creating a *Service with Purpose* company is a rewarding and fulfilling process and that the work you do with this positive business strategy will help to make customer service a habit and not just an act for you and your employees.

Wow, I hope you're ready to go because I'm down to my last few words. This is my last chance to encourage you to go for it and to let you know that you really can do this. It *will* work for you. So don't wait to start becoming a *Service with Purpose* company. Take action today – right now! Action above all will provide you with the success you deserve. Go for it!

Good Luck and enjoy the journey to becoming a *Service with Purpose* superstar!

Epilogue

You've read a great deal about my philosophies and techniques for bringing a caring approach to your business. You've hopefully begun to set some high standards for yourself based on the words within this book. But until you take action and start adopting the philosophies that will make a difference, this book is nothing more than a collection of meaningless words.

So before I leave you to create your *Service with Purpose* magic, I want to stand behind my words and my beliefs in a way that can reach out to you. I want to make the connection right now – as you're reading these words – to the power of caring. After all, I can talk about caring all I want, but all that really matters is whether or not I "walk the walk."

Therefore, I want to end this book by introducing you to an incredible organization that exists today because of the caring of those who operate it and those who help to fund it. I am proud to say that by purchasing this book you have helped to make a sick child's dream come true. With every book sold, a small contribution will be made to Give Kids The World, a fantastic place near Orlando, Florida. I hope that in the months and years to come, you'll find that Give Kids The World is worthy of your continued support.

The organization was founded by Henri Landwirth, a successful Central Florida hotelier, who had offered accommodations to a young girl suffering from leukemia and her family. However, he was deeply saddened to learn that time had proved the enemy in the race to finalize a multitude of arrangements for the trip. The girl died without experiencing her wish.

Mr. Landwirth immediately called upon colleagues in the hospitality industry – including theme parks – to assist him with a project to bring families to Central Florida with less than 24 hours notice, if the situation called for such action. Before long, Mr. Landwirth and two staff members began arranging wish vacations out of a converted storeroom in one of his hotels. He named this fledgling organization after its mission, "Give Kids The World," because that is what he intended to do.

Mr. Landwirth called upon friends from the early days of his career as a hotel manager in Cocoa Beach, and Give Kids The World Village opened its gates to welcome its first families in early 1989. His friends answered his call and his vision became a reality.

Today, the Village features nearly 100 villas, a whimsical restaurant, magical play area, an ice cream palace, a movie theatre, an interactive waterpark, a fishing pond, and even a peaceful chapel. Each year, the Village welcomes families from communities in all 50 states and from more than 47 countries. And with the contributions and support of caring businesses and caring individuals, Give Kids The World helps more children with each passing year.

From the very first family who visited to the families that are arriving at the gates of the Village today, thousand of families a year have enjoyed a few precious days away from hospitals, doctor visits, and medical treatments. They thrive in an environment filled with laughter, joy and hugs.

And it all began because one little girl's dream touched the heart of a man who cared.

What else can I say – caring makes all the difference in the world. If that's the only message you take from this book then it was all worthwhile.

For more information, you can find a link to the Give Kids The World homepage on www.ServiceWithPurpose.com

The Six Essentials of Service

1 - Vision

2 - Hiring

3 - Training

4 - Communication

5 - Recognition

6 - Revision

Bibliography
(and recommended reading)

Blanchard, Ken, and Sheldon Bowles. High Five! The Magic of Working Together. N.p.: William Morrow, 2000.

Blanchard, Ken, and Sheldon Bowles. Raving Fans: A Revolutionary Approach To Customer Service. N.p.: William Morrow, 1993.

Blanchard, Ken. Gung Ho! Turn On The People in Any Organization. N.p.: William Morrow, 1997.

Blanchard, Kenneth, et al. Whale Done! The Power of Positive Relationships. N.p.: Free P, 2002.

Capodagli, Bill, and Lynn Jackson. The Disney Way: Harnessing the Management Secrets of Disney in Your Company. N.p.: McGraw-Hill, 1999.

Carlson, Jan. Moments of Truth. Cambridge, Mass.: Ballinger Co., 1987.

Connellan, Tom. Inside The Magic Kingdom: Seven Keys to Disney's Success. Austin, TX: Bard P, 1997.

Disney Institute. Be Our Guest. New York: Disney Editions, 2001.

Fournies, Ferdinand F. Coaching for Improved Work Performance. N.p.: McGraw-Hill, 2000.

Gitomer, Jeffrey. Customer Satisfaction is Worthless, Customer Loyalty is Priceless. N.p.: Bard P, 1998.

Griffin, Jill. Customer Loyalty - How to Earn It How to Keep It. San Francisco: Jossey-Bass, 1995.

Gross, T. Scott. Positively Outrageous Service. New York: Master Media Ltd., 1991.

Lundin, Stephen, et al. Fish! A Remarkable Way to Boost Morale and Improve Results. N.p.: Hyperion P, 2000.

Nelson, Bob. 1001 Ways to Reward Employees. N.p.: Workman Co., 1994.

Olney, Timothy M. Life Positive. N.p.: Leaderbook, 2001.

Reichheld, Frederick F., and Thomas Teal. The Loyalty Effect: The Hidden Force Behind Growth, Profits, and Lasting Value. N.p.: Harvard Business School P, 2001.

Weinstein, Matt. Managing To Have Fun. New York: Simon & Schuster, 1996.

About the Author...

Scott Brown has been studying, developing and practicing his customer service strategies and philosophies for over 15 years. He has compiled his years of experience in his first book, *Who Cares? Creating a Culture of Service in your Business.*

Scott is a graduate of the College of Journalism and Communication at the University of Florida. He has published several articles on the subject of customer service and management. In addition to being an author, Scott is also a speaker helping businesses and individuals reach their service potential.

Scott lives in Ohio with his wife, Susan, and two daughters – Savannah and Delaney.

If you would like Scott to speak to your group or organization, or if you would like more information on Scott or his services, please visit his website at: www.ServiceWithPurpose.com

Note from the author

Customer service is my passion. For so many of us, our businesses or our jobs are a huge part of our lives. By embracing an attitude of outstanding service to our co-workers and our customers, we have a way to positively impact the lives of others. If you have any *Service with Purpose* stories or strategies you'd like to share or ideas for future books, I'd love to hear them. E-mail me!

scott@sbservicepro.com

Order Additional Copies of *Who Cares?*

Would you like to share additional copies of *Who Cares?* with your clients, co-workers or management team? There are three ways to contact us to order.

- Visit us on-line at
    www.ServiceWithPurpose.com
- Fax your order to 1-330-335-7809
- Or if you prefer you can still do it the old-fashioned way. You can use the order form provided and mail it to the address at the bottom of the page.

YES! I want _____ copies of *Who Cares?* at $14.95 each, plus $3 shipping & handling per book. (Ohio residents, please add 6% sales tax.) Be sure to also include a contact name, shipping address and phone number.

Quantity discounts are available

My check or money order for $_____ is enclosed.

Send this form to: Savadel Publishing
                          P.O. Box 121
                          Sharon Center, Ohio 44274